Stories of
Life and Death

Stories of Life and Death

Juan Ramón Jiménez

Translation by
Antonio T. de Nicolás

Illustrated by
Martin Hardy

toExcel
San Jose New York Lincoln Shanghai

Stories of Life and Death

Published by toExcel
an imprint of iUniverse.com, Inc.

For information address:
iUniverse.com, Inc.
620 North 48th Street
Suite 201
Lincoln, NE 68504-3467
www.iuniverse.com

ISBN: 0-595-00269-2

Printed in the United States of America

Contents

Translator's
Dedication

YOU CAME TO ME with a sudden gift,
your eyes green meadows
your lap overflowing
with red carnations and white roses.

You came to me with a sudden gift,
clean sunrises in lips
softly parted at the break
of foam arising uncontained
from the distant depths of a young
sea timidly surging to embrace
in thousand waves the hard shore.

You came to me with a sudden gift
and the answer was to think
the price of gifts that bear
no tag and soften the rock of a man's
heart because they have no price.

You came to me with a sudden gift
that froze in me as winter and
you were gone and left no reason
to learn not to question spring.
Death is the heart's season.

Acknowledgements

I wish to thank,
Louis Simpson, true poet, true friend, for his encouragement,
and for forcing me to read Rilke. Mary Bruno for her dedicated
effort to make these stories more readable.

Juan Ramón Jiménez: A Poet of Life and Death

by Antonio T. de Nicolás

Juan Ramón Jiménez (1881–1958) has contributed more to contemporary poetry than, perhaps, any other poet. Even though he received the Nobel Prize for Literature in 1956 his name is not well known in English literary circles. This lack of recognition is partly due to the fact that so little of the poet's work exists in English. The present translations are an effort to correct this situation.

The present selection of his work, gathered under the title *Stories of Life and Death,* is both an extention of and a preparation for the poet's better known prose/poetry work *Platero y Yo (Platero and I).* Perhaps more than his other writings, these selections deal directly with the eternal paradoxes of poetry: its universal message and its individual origins; its eternal hankering after life and its constant reminder of death; its message of joy and its dedication to sadness; its individual voice and its public recognition of universal experience; its individual elegy and its life-sustaining plasma for the human species. These are tempting paradoxes and few poets arrange them as temptingly as Juan Ramón Jiménez.

I did not want, however, to theorize on poetry without discussing the space of poetry which the poet creates through composition. My translation shares this recreation, or as Juan Ramón would have said, at "confirmation." "All correction," translation, he wrote in his *Epigrams,* "is a confirmation."

Poetic Space

In 1956 Anders Osterling, in the name of the Swedish Academy, granted Juan Ramón the Nobel Prize for Literature, noting that the prize was, "A tribute to Spanish Literature, which for various reasons had had little fortune in these international competitions. . ." He added: "By being an idealist dreamer, Juan Ramón Jiménez represents . . . the highest Spanish tradition and honoring him is also to honor Antonio Machado and Garciá Lorca, his disciples who praised him as their master." The official papers granting the Nobel Prize proclaimed: "For your lyric poetry, which in the Spanish language, constitutes an exemplar of high spirituality and artistic purity." (*Libros de Poesias* 1959, vii).

Here we face the first paradox. Juan Ramón Jiménez received the news of the Nobel Prize in almost the same circumstances in which he wrote his poetry—by the bedside of death. His beloved wife, Zenobia, was dying. The poet survived her by only two years. When the poet stops creating to become an exemplar of culture and tradition, the poet silences his private voice and dies. Apparently the artistic and creative achievement is in the journey, not the arrival.

"Love and poetry everyday," Juan Ramón wrote as the motto of his work *Eternidades*. When his love ceased so did his poetry. And herein lies the next paradox. Someone besides the poet must resurrect his work from the ashes of death.

I read Juan Ramón Jiménez while in a crisis of passage from childhood into adolescence. *Platero y Yo* was placed in my hands without promises or apologies. Within its pages I discovered a new world which I could only call love. Love emanated from the pages and, as a consequence, the world appeared different. Within that new world I discovered my most treasured secret, the space of poetry.

Passages from *Platero y Yo* followed me everywhere: "Everyone has gone to church. The sparrows, Platero and I have stayed in the garden." And these: "Everyone, even the guard, has left for town to see the procession. Platero and I have been left all alone. What peace! What purity! What well being!" And this: "Loneliness is like one large thought of light."

Poets went to a secret place to create poetry. This space of poetry was separate from othres. Loneliness was not a state of being, it was the condition to enter the space of creation. The philosophical questions came later. Was this space private? Or did we all inhabit it, but only the poet mediated the private into the universal? Did our participation in solitude make poetry the universal public experience we all recognize? Was poetry, really, the private experience, or rather was it only through poetry that the human species recognized its common and public face?

In time I learned to recognize the solitary space of poetry, where death and memory play the eternal ritual. From death

rises the promise of eternal life, yet decay and death are what
we feel. The death the poet fears is oblivion. True death only
occurs where human memory does not reach. Whatever
humans forget is forever dead. That is why Rilke may
dispassionately sing:

> I have my dead, and I have let them go,
> and was amazed to see them so contented,
> so soon at home in being dead, so cheerful,
> so unlike their reputation. . . .

Rilke also reminds us that between the revival of
memories the indifference of life brings impassive affection to
the ardor of our desires. Because our desires are not aimed at
resurrection of the dead but at self gratification, our limits are
the angel and the puppet:

> Angel and puppet: a real play, finally.

The angel is self sufficient desire, the puppet is bestowed
affection impassively unreturned. Between angel and puppet
the poet carves his space of creation: Following those
footsteps we shall enter the space of poetry.

*　*　*　*

Juan Ramón Jiménez was born in Moguer, Province of
Huelva, Andalucía, on Christmas Eve 1881. In his
autobiographical notes, which appeared in the magazine
Renacimiento and later in *Libros de Poesías,* 1959 he wrote:
"My father was Castillian and had blue eyes; my mother
Andalusian and had black eyes. The white marvel of my village
wrapped my infancy within an old house with large rooms and
green patios. I remember from these sweet years that I played
very little and liked being alone; solemnities, visits, churches
filled me with fear." By the age of eleven Juan Ramón became

an intern in the Jesuit School in Puerto de Santa María. "My eleventh year entered in mourning . . . leaving behind my feelings: the window through which I watched the rain fall in the garden, my forest, the sun setting on my street." But soon he discovered continuity: "Next to my bedroom there was a window overlooking the beach and where on Spring nights I could watch the deep sky asleep over the sea, and in the distance, Cadiz with the sad light of a lighthouse."

That space began to take wider shape when the poet left school: "There was something happy in my life: Love appeared in my path." At the appearance of love, the poet began to write and be published. His writing and reading Becquer, Byron, Espronceda, Heine, Verlaine, Samain, Göethe, Hölderlin, Keats, Shelley, Browning, Shakespeare, Poe, Petrarch, Carducci, D'Annunzio, the Spanish classics, and one philosopher Plato, made him indifferent to the fact that he was unable to get through law school. His health began to deteriorate, but as he wrote: "This was such a happy time of my life I became indifferent to science and to death." An interesting footnote to this period is that Juan Ramón started his artistic life not as a poet but as a painter in Sevilla. His style was impressionistic, and his writing preserved this vision. His early writings published in Sevilla, were recognized by the poets of Madrid, Rubén Darío and Francisco Villaespesa, who invited Juan Ramón to join the literary circle around the magazine *Vida Nueva*. At eighteen, in April 1900 Juan Ramón joined the Spanish and international literary life. As his fame increased, his health deteriorated.

His father died: "The death of my father covered my soul with a dark obsession . . . . I became afraid of death, of sudden death; only the presence of a doctor would bring me rest . . . I became filled with a disquieting mysticism that overtook me completely. I attended processions and tore to pieces a whole book I had written—*Besos de Oro*—for I considered it too profane." Juan Ramón started a pilgrimage through sanatoriums. The first was at Castel d'Amdorte in Le Bouscat, Bordeaux, France. There, in the garden, he wrote *Rimas* at the age of twenty. Homesick for Spain he returned to Madrid in 1901 and entered the Sanatorium El Rosario. There he spent, in his words: "Two of the best years of my life, some sensuous religiosity, the peace of the cloister, the smell of incense and flowers, a window overlooking the garden and a terrace with rosebushes for those nights with moonlight . . ." *Jardines Lejanos* (1905), *Palabras Románticas* (1905), *Olvidanzas* (1905) followed.

Suddenly he became preoccupied with finances and obsessed with death. A new pilgrimage from doctor to clinic, from clinic to laboratories followed. He felt: "Cold, tired, inclined to suicide and once again the countryside wraps me up within its spring . . . Now, in this life of loneliness and meditation between village and countryside, with the silver rosebush of experience in bloom, I feel the greatest indifference towards life; all I am left with as food for my soul is the beauty that feeds my heart in the form of an eternal elegy." This eternal elegy is the "inner form" of the poetic space.

Between 1907 and 1911 Juan Ramón lived in the countryside ("I am each day more within my life and less within literature,") and wrote *Poemas Májicos y dolientes, Melancolía, Laberinto* and his most memorable piece *Platero y Yo.* Between 1913 and 1916 the poet returned to Madrid, met Zenobia his future wife, and wrote *Sonetos Espirituales, Estío,* and *Diario de un poeta recíen casado*—the story of his marriage and honeymoon in the United States and return to Spain. From then on the poet retreated deeper into his inner, solitary place, while his poetry became freer and more original. With his book *Eternidades* (1918) a new period opened for the writer. One year later *Piedra y Cielo* appeared.

At this point Juan Ramón worked on translations of Rabindranath Tagore and collaborated on anthologies of his work *Poesías Escojidas* (1899–1912), *Segunda Antología*

Poética (1989–1918). Between 1926 and 1936 his major poetic works were written, *La estacíon total.* In 1942 his second prose work appeared, *Españoles de Tres Mundos.* The Spanish Civil War interrupted the poetic creation until 1949 when his work *Animal de Fondo* was published in Argentina, as part of his poem *Dios deseado y deseante,* which remains unfinished to this day.

In 1933 when he left Spain for America he wrote:

> I have hardly looked at the water, the sea. My being my body and soul are not (on this second voyage to America so different from the first) with this present, tranquil sea, so stupidly tranquil, but with my distant land that has gone crazy (*Diario poético*).

The elegy reappeared as soon as he arrived in New York for the second time:

> Twenty years ago New York had visible flesh and soul.
> Today all of it is already a machine (*Libros de Poésia,* xxiv).

The poet summed up his life thus:

> My life has been a constant jump, a revolution, a permanent shipwreck. Moguer, Puerto de Santa Maria, Moguer, Sevilla, Moguer, Madrid, Moguer, France, Madrid, Moguer, Madrid, America, Madrid, America . . . And in America, New York, Puerto Rico, Florida, Washington, Argentina, Puerto Rico, Maryland, Puerto Rico . . . And in every place to start again, start again, start again! (*Libros de Poesías, xxvi*).

This external "start again," trained the poet for his internal "start again." The poet straddles the common experience where both meet: death. As he said when he saw his wife die: "The only truth is death." (*Libros de Poesías, xxvii*) even though this truth is not logical, it is more universal than any logical truth. The poet is its guardian:

> It is not life that must fear
> death, but rather death.
> The living that has passed,
> has not yet passed,
> as the day we were born is not yet over,
> nor the dream we have dreamed, nor the rose
> we smelled, nor the embrace we received,
> nor the book we read.
> The past is not dead,
> ruins live,
> dead, we shall live in death,
> if we live
> as long as life shall live.
> It is not our life that dies,
> what has been will never die,
> what dies is only death.

> (in *Circle of Paradox*, 167–68; my translation. 1967.
> Paul R. Olson, *Circle of Paradox*, The Johns
> Hopkins University Press: Baltimore.)

This is the ultimate paradox of poetry. In order to keep a secret poetry must make it public. This public mission turns the best poets into searchers for the best way to spread the word. Poets change styles, rhymes, use free verse or even prose as in the case of Juan Ramón.

Reading poetry, Juan Ramón realized, was a habit acquired by a small minority. He wrote poetry in prose so that his poetic message would reach an "immense minority" to whom he dedicated his writings (*Estetica y Etica estética,* 47). His style influenced the writer-poets who followed him, *Impressiones y Paisajes* (1918) by Federico García Lorca; *Oscuro Domino* (1934) by Juan Larrea; *Pasión de la Tierra* (1935) and *Los encuentros* (1958) by the other Spanish Nobel Laureate Vicente Aleixandre; and *Ocnos* (1942) and *Variaciones sobre Temas Mejicanos* (1952) by Luis Cernuda.

Juan Ramón Jiménez's life spans fifty years of work dedicated to poetry, in verse, in free verse and in prose. His secret is very simple: poetry is death, to live in death is the only way to live fully. The poems, in prose or verse, of Juan Ramón, have no other message. The information one would expect from prose is absent; instead Juan Ramón focuses on sensations. He conveys the sensations of the eye, the ear, touch, movement, smell in a manner closer to impressionistic painting than to the written word. He minimizes the obvious and enlarges the essential to convey the eternal. The poet's senses die with the arousal of sensation. Where life rises, death follows. The poet witnesses this transition which happens in his soul. For this reason Juan Ramón's different styles are inseparable. He is the complete poet, the poet who as he said, "has jailed poetry in his own home." What he expresses in whatever form, is poetry. He claimed that the test of this statement would be to read his poetry, in verse or prose, to a blind person. The blind person would certainly understand (*Historias y Cuentos,* 13). Gustavo Adolfo Bécquer would have agreed because he also believed that poetry is the reader. Poet and reader form a communion only if the experience holding them together is common, as in death.

Death and Poetry

Literary critics would have us believe that a universal reader could be created on condition that we abstract the living time of the poet and make his creation fit some universal logic. The second coming of Don Quixote is at hand, this time in search of theoretical windmills. Only, this time he talks to himself, Sancho Panza is not allowed to enter the conversation . The poet does not demand that we believe anything, but only that we read his or her writings. The poet rests on an experience of death common to both poet and reader.

How many sunsets must burn for one to become eternal through the words of the poet? How many loves must be lost, how many accepted, how many denied, how many fade for one to become poetic, eternal word? How many lights, and how many shadows must struggle through words, names, adjectives, and pain to form that space of poetic discourse through which poets and readers transcend their individual boundaries and become universal? Juan Ramón wrote:

> Let us create names,
> Men will drift away,
> Then, things will follow them,
> There will remain only the world of names,
> Words of the love of humans,
> Of the fragrance of roses.
> Of love and roses,
> Only names will remain,
> Let us create names!

But the names must be the exact, must be created new:

> Intellect, give me
> the exact name of things!
> Let my word be
> The thing itself,
> newly created by my soul.

The creation of the language of poetry is the life of the poet:

Eternal word of mine!
Oh, the supreme living.

What is death that the poet chooses as his supreme living? Here we face one of the paradoxes of poetry. While most people give little thought to death, except when there is a death in the family, the poet appropriates the immediacy of death and turns it into universal, common experience through poetic language. Poetic language by arousing creates a common memory in the reader, forgotten thoughts. Through poetic language the poet creates a living memory for the reader.

Not all poets, however, use death as does Juan Ramón with the same softness of voice and the same results. For example Rainer Maria Rilke, who wrote his *Duino Elegies* while Juan Ramón was writing some of the entries in *Stories of Life and Death,* is the most obvious contrast:

> Murderers are easy
> to understand. But this, that one can contain
> death, the whole of death, even before
> life was begun, can hold it to one's heart
> gently, and not refuse to go on living,
> is inexpressible (*Fourth Elegy*).

One cannot help but hear the harsh, loud voice of the poet not reconciled with witnessing death while recounting it:

> But we, when moved by deep feelings, evaporate;
> we breathe ourselves out and away; from
> moment to moment our emotion grows fainter,
> life a perfume. Though someone may tell us
> "yes, you've entered my bloodstream, the
> room, the whole springtime is filled with
> you . . ."—what does it matter? He can't

contain us, we vanish inside and around him.
And those who are beautiful, O, who can retain
them? Appearance ceaselessly rises in their
face, and is gone. Like dew from the morning
grass, what is ours floats into the air, like steam
from a dish of hot food. O smile, where are you
going? O upturned glance: new warm receding
wave on the sea of the heart . . . Alas, but that
is what we are. Does the infinite space we
dissolve into, taste of us then? . . . (*First
Elegy*).

This is the daily bread of human experience. Love rises,
emotion, feeling, elation rise, but simultaneously decay begins.
Love frays, emotions change, feelings fall, highs become lows,
every inner move is a new receding wave on the sea of the
human heart. The true poet follows these footsteps of death,
lives them and turns them into poetry. Poets differ in their
attitude to reminding us of human decay. Some surrender to it
with more grace, loving it and turning it into common joy;
others resent it and reject it, yet are unable to cancel its
message. Rilke's voice remains always sharper, louder,
accusing:

Lovers, gratified in each other, I am asking you
about us. You hold each other. Where is your
proof?

Again we face another paradox of poetry. The poet does
not have to like his life even when the message he delivers is
his choice. Plato, when he writes in his *Republic* the Journey of
Er, reminds us that the witness of death—philosopher, poet, or
simple messenger—does so at his own risk. He is not chosen
by anyone for this task. The gods have no life for him. These
humans find the angel terrifying. The absolute fulfillment of the

angel is outside the reach of the poet. The poet cannot stand the puppet either for the puppet represents his passions and feelings. The puppets receive them impassively, indifferently, like the angel. In the absence of both angel and puppet, death remains the messenger from the dead. Where life appears in discontinuous fashion, death appears in stubborn continuity. The language of poetry is the narration of this continuity of death, of the common ground of humanity. Through death humans leave their individuality to establish their presence in the human race. The poet is the narrator, the witness, the messenger of this presence. Without the message, human memory would die.

Juan Ramón Jiménez speaks with a different voice. Not only does he seem at home in accepting the message, he also enjoys the role of messenger. Perhaps Juan Ramón was luckier than others in his love experiences. He did not have to share his love as Rilke did. Perhaps the constant presence of love helped him to purify his heart from exaggerated, private delusions. He wrote in soft tones:

> My heart is now so pure,
> it is the same whether
> it sings or dies.
>
> I can fill the book of life,
> or the book of death;
> both are blank
> for those who think or dream.
>
> I will find eternity in birth.
> Heart! It is the same: die or sing.

Juan Ramón experienced a cosmic relationship with the universe, and he felt as one with the human species. His voice does not sound individual, rebellious or even heroic. Juan

Ramón's voice is voice of death, if death ever had a voice, the ever present, ever calm, ever universal, ever joyful voice in its daily task of becoming human through language, memory, and imagination.

> Come! Give me your presence
> for you die if you die
> in me . . . and forget you!
> Come, come to me, for I wish to give you life
> with my memory, while I die!

This concept of the cosmic presence of death as the source of life is closer to the East than to the West. In the East death is viewed as continuous, life as discontinuous. Hinduism and Buddhism teach that the appearance of life is only the occasion for acknowledging the continuity of death. In death we are all eternal and present. Humans come from death—continuity—in order to accumulate life—discontinuity—and return to continuity. (This is a different concept than that of being born and moving towards death. Juan Ramón Jiménez accepts this concept when in his self portrait in "El Andaluz Universal" (The Universal Andalusian) he claimed his roots were Oriental, while his birth was geographically Spanish:

> You, then, come out of death dry and silent,
> Like the flaming spark from the stone, silent,
> Like the endless scent from the bark, dry,
> Like the pure dripping of the stagnant pond, dead.

The signs of life are only signs of the individual's death:

> This infinite poison
> so saturates the flowers
> one desires,
> it kills us!

Poison of light and foam
able only in life
to give life to others,
and bring death to us!

Individual, discontinuous life transcends itself and
becomes universal and eternal in death. Death devours time
and transforms it into eternity and universality. Language
provides the inner technology of this transformation through
ordering memories and imaginings. Through language, poetry
forces the invisible to become visible and public.

It is irresponsible to label what we do not understand as
either Oriental or mystical. Juan Ramón may have found his
poetic tradition in the Spanish classics which in turn derived
from the tradition of Plato. I have spent many years writing on
both eastern subjects and western philosophy and have
repeatedly said that Plato is the largest footnote we have to
previous cultures. Plato embodies the continuity of the past
and our own discontinuity.

Plato, our first literary critic and who remains
unsurpassed to this day, was probably the only philosopher
Juan Ramón read and certainly the only one he followed.

Plato wrote against poets who imitate discrete objects
and hide their lack of true poetry in the ability to rhyme. Plato
also wrote against poets who expend energy getting rid of the
dead. On both counts Homer was his favorite bad poet. True
creation, for Plato, is possible only in the presence of death.

In the first five books of the *Republic* Plato tries to form a
community of young men who define justice on condition that
they "saw" it first. When this fails Plato introduces, in the sixth
book, *the divided line*. On this line he makes two cuts: one
larger than the other, one named "intelligible," the other
"visible." Together both cuts embraced all knowledge and
training required of any Athenian citizen in the position to
make decisions for the rest of society. The shorter part of the

divided line included opinions, images derived from objects, and objects derived from the sciences and the arts. The longer part of the line contained all else: creation from nothing, creation from imagining. Plato did not indicate which part of the divided line was the visible and which the intelligible.

When his audience failed to understand that both are essential to the Republic, Plato introduced a dramatic shock. He moved his audience to the "cave" where Plato/Socrates demonstrates that intelligibles only cast shadows. When his audience still did not fully understand, he moved then again, with the exception of the logician Thrasymachus, to the presence of death. There, in the presence of death he narrated the Journey of Er. Er was a Pamphilian, a foreigner who made his home everywhere. Through Er, Plato rewrote Homer. The Hector that Homer buried in the *Iliad* is not dead in the *Republic* of Plato/Socrates. Hector is resurrected by Plato/Socrates in order to make visible and present the history and images of the past. Plato does not name Achilles in the *Republic* and thus he holds back forever the hand that killed memory.

Memory must keep death alive, imagining must be used to reconstruct the death of the past through language that extends memory and imagining beyond the limits of individual burials. The poet builds through language, memory, and imaginings living world that becomes new footsteps for other mortals to remember and imagine. The poet is the master of the technologies of the visible.

It is not, therefore, enough to quote some statements of Juan Ramón calling himself simply a follower of Plato: "I am, was, and will be a Platonist," as he wrote to Luis Cernuda in 1943 (*La Corriente Infinita*, 1961), or that he accepted Plato's definition of poetry as he wrote in *Caracola* in 1954:

> Until an unsuspected miracle appears to tell us
> something better, I accept the ancient
> definition (of poetry) by Plato. Yes, for me

poetry is something divine, winged, full of grace, expression of the charm and mystery of the world. (Divine, here, means original, primal, since God in his name is nothing but beginning and origin (*La Corriente Infinita,* Madrid: 1961, 218).)

What is significant is to see Juan Ramón using memory, imagining, and language as prescribed as Plato.

This instant
which has already become memory, what is it?
Mad music,
which brings these colors that were not
—for they belong
to that evening of gold, love and glory;
this music
moving towards not being, what is it?
Instant, move on, be memory
—memory, you are more, for you cross
death endlessly with your arrow—,
be memory, with me already gone!
Oh, yes, move on, move on to be not an instant,
but eternity in memory!
Immense memory of mine,
of moments passed centuries ago;
eternity of the soul of death!
. . . Instant, move on, move on, you who are
—alas!—myself!
This instant, this you,
which is about to be by dying, what is it?
(*Libros de Poesías,* 702–3)

In *Stories of Life and Death* the poet, the painter, the critic, the external and the internal relate more explicitly to that "inner center." Each story is built on death, the death of a child, the death of a blade of grass, the death of human grace, the death of all that comes to life. "How sad was that bit of sun hanging over the cemetery when they carried you there dead," the stories begin. But then the poet plays with the little girls: "In my exuberance I turned to the little girls . . . What peace and joy! Sweet vibrant bells sang in the open sunset. Every turn of the breeze let out a new scent, which then got lost very deep in the soul . . ." And finally: "I stayed by myself, in the tiny orchard, among shadows. The orchard also turned solitary and cold."

Juan Ramón is a master at catching the precise instant that separates life and death. Describing a dormitory with children asleep all around: "Suddenly two large magnetic eyes were staring at me, shining, fixed, like black burning coals . . . Those eyes, no doubt were open long before I was able to see them; they were eyes fixed upon themselves, with no relation to others . . . (those eyes were) rather the one and only true death." True death is also the love of a child "now dry, though it beat so much and so uselessly for us." Or the child abandoned in a clearing to play pointing fingers at the moon, or the secret love of the bad poet for his teacher, or the black child who wanted to look whiter, or the blind young men of Madrid who only hold opinions if others share them, or that absent sister who kept the heart of a drunk and miserable man clean with only her memory, or the old invalid unable to watch the carnival, for "from his sleep to death there is no more distance than half a meter of tiredness," or the young Filipino girl who felt as a stranger where she lived.

When the gaze of the poet turns sideways, the effect is exhilarating. He sees people's profiles, their double identities; women stealing from each other their graces and cancelling each other's personalities; the flesh of old age and the eyes of the young, the gaze of innocence and the glances of the demented, the eyes of love and those of deception. He sees the world. And while the reader sees this world with the poet, at times simple at times baroque, a thread of common memories unite the act of reading to that of writing. The memory of the reader moved by agility of the writer responds to new worlds of imagination. This stimulus to imagination is the reward of reading *Stories of Life and Death.*

About the Present Translation

Juan Ramón Jiménez considered his writing as work on the go, "*una obra en marcha.*" He announced on several occasions books which never appeared, though parts were published within other books or anthologies or under different titles. Even the book *Platero y Yo* was published in a first edition in 1914, a longer one in 1917 and the author labored until 1934 to bring out a new edition of the same work with a different ordering of the episodes and with new entries. This project was never completed. While Juan Ramón was alive only two books written in prose, besides *Platero y Yo,* were published, *Españoles de Tres Mundos* (1942) and *El Zaratán* (1946). The present translation is based on material published under the Spanish title of *Historias y Cuentos* (Bruguera: Barcelona, 1979). The stories were written during the years from 1900 to 1952. The Spanish editors have gathered these entries under four main themes: Golden Age (Stories About Children); Compassionate Shoulder (Friendly Hand); Long Stories; and Natural Crimes. Since Juan Ramón had the fastidious habit of constantly correcting and recorrecting his writings, the dates written under the entries are only approximate. Where there are two dates, the first indicates the date of composition and the other the date of final correction. The Spanish editors had to resolve many problems for the ordering of the present edition, but as Auturo del Villar writes in his Spanish Introduction: "the readers of this collection will discover that the prose of Juan Ramón is as beautiful as that of *Platero y Yo,* as affirmative as that of *Españoles de Tres Mundos* and as exact as that of his poems."

Unlike *Platero y Yo*, however, *Stories of Life and Death* have no overriding connection. These stories are self contained; each one lives and dies on its own. They do not depend for their effect on a main character. The reader may start reading anywhere. Juan Ramón's prose is as exact as his poetry, his economy of language produces the greatest impressionistic effect. This creates a problem for the translator because in English little is taken for granted and everything must appear on the written page. Some entries, in particular, should be told in one single breath. In Spanish the sentence moves without punctuation with the inner movement of a wave surging towards the shore of shared understanding of author and reader. In English this effort reads like a plurality of run-on sentences. To achieve clarity in translation, I slowed the surging wave with punctuation, or broke it into smaller waves.

Musicality is the inner rhythm of Juan Ramón's language, whether verse, free verse, or prose. This translation is biased towards the musical rhythm of Spanish rather than the logical grammar of English. I have tried to translate the reader to Juan Ramón's spaces of musical discourse rather than translate Juan Ramón into English spaces of logical discourse. I tried to preserve the "otherness" of Spanish.

Antonio T. de Nicolás,
Setauket 1985

Prefatory Poems

The poems of Juan Ramón Jiménez presented in this section are designed as an exercise to better prepare the reader for the stories that follow.

My heart is now so pure,

it is the same whether

it sings or dies.

I can fill the book of life,

or the book of death,

both are blank

for those who think or dream.

I will find eternity in birth.

Heart! It is the same: die or sing.

Be the Eternal Birth

Be the eternal birth

which gathers the dying lavender sun,

each instant, in the sunset of my life!

Ideal Epitaph
For a Heart That Stopped

Rosebushes grow now

where his faith rested.

They go where his faith went

(where did it go?):

spring scents.

Come, Give Me Your Presence

Come! Give me your presence,
for you die if you die
in me . . . and forget you!
Come, come to me, for I wish to give you life
with my memory, while I die!

Chalice

This infinite poison
so saturates the flowers
one desires,
it kills us!

Poison of light and foam
able only in life
to give life to others,
and to bring death to us!

Epitaph for a Young Man
He Died in Spring.

He died. But do not cry for him!
Does not April return each year,
naked, bloomed, singing
on its white horse?

You, Then, Came Out of Death

You, then, came out of death dry and silent,
Like the flaming spark from the stone, silent,
Like the endless scent from the bark, dry,
Like the pure dripping of the stagnant pond, dead.

Ideal Epitaph for a Woman Who Died in a Novel

You are here. It's only
that your soul climbed to the most noble.
It's only—you are here—
the blossoming of a day, sad and brief.

Dead

His weight remained fixed:
one scale in the mud,
one scale in the sky.

I Know Well I Am the Trunk

I know well I am the trunk
of the tree of the Eternal.
I know well I feed the stars
with the sap of my blood,
that all clear dreams
are birds of mine . . .
I know well that when the ax
of death fells me,
the skies will tumble down.

Ideal Epitaph to a Hero

He reached his death. But his living
was so intense, that though he lies here rotting
destiny watches, still, over him.

Nocturne

I will kiss you in the shade
my body not touching
your body.
—I will draw the curtains,
that not even the mist of heaven
may enter—.
   In the absolute death of everything
may my kiss, oh new world,
be the only thing that exists.

How Well My Soul Dwells in My Body

How well my soul dwells in my body
—like a unique idea
within a perfect verse—
and yet I must go and leave
the body—like a rhetorician's verse—
useless and dead!

Blessed He That Is Born

Blessed he that is born
on the eve of the end, he that hears
the last melody, he that plucks
the last flower from feeling,
the last light from thought!

What a true death
to the truth of here, no more desire!
Oh, what a joyous entry
into your honey, the all, perhaps yours, nothing!

Dream, Dream While You Sleep

Dream, dream while you sleep!
You will forget it with the coming day.

Day, blissful training
of infinite wisdom!

Learn, learn while awake;
You will forget it sleeping.

Sleep, blissful training
of the definitive oblivion!

The Dead Woman

You have not left. It's only that before,
body and soul united,
you moved within the world.

But now (you have not left),
body and soul so distant,
the world moves between you.

Epitaph to Myself, Alive

I died in sleep,
I woke up in life.

Part I

The Golden Age

(Stories About Children)

I

The Dead Little Girl

1.

How sad was that bit of sun hanging over the cemetery when they carried you there dead. A rose was lighting up in it, the birds chased its warmth, and as the sun climbed the branches of the acacia tree, the birds climbed with it. It finally became just a lyric and melodious golden dome. By then your box was turning blue in the humid shadow; your path, now without your return—and with mine, so sad!—felt cold. And the children who were running behind your white box—dawns in the sad afternoon—were looking at you in astonishment at the door of your new home. The son of the grave digger was eating bread and butter, unconcerned.

2.

As I entered the room, now dark, to hand over the little key of the white box to her mother, the sun, outside, was still sweetening with gold the pear trees of the corral and the sparrows were still singing in the eaves of the roofs and the afternoon sky was uselessly pouring simultaneously down the roses and gold of dreams in a lyric, pagan and musical cleanliness!

3.

The little girl had a golden canary, one of those that looks like a coin of gold—fresh, joyful and hopping. His cage was by the garden window, against a background of green, of flower with sun, with plenty of blue sky—that large sky of the villages!—with the fields resting on the last roofs. He knew the little girl as if she had been born with him in the same nest; he would jump on her hand, his beak extended, his wings folded; he would talk to her with his best music; he would laugh. The little girl would carry the cage to a table where she would stand on a chair and shower the little bird with playfulness and love.

On the afternoon the little girl fell ill, the bird buried under his wing his tiny head of white gold. He stopped eating, drinking, or bathing in the crystal jar, nor did he curl his silvery gold against the fine wire. Such things! Yes, I know! Nothing . . . A coincidence. Absurd . . . Yes, I know, but. . . .

The little girl died—with a sadness that made us all cry, and her mother: "How sad you leave, my daughter!"—with those large eyes now blind turning towards the loved voices, the familiar steps, every sound, every caress, every sigh. When we set down the little girl in the white box, upon so many flowers, I left to cry with the sad bird, the one soul in the house most like mine. Stiff, a wing in the air, he lay at the bottom of the cage, which suddenly seemed to me to be empty, though the dead bird was in it.

What golden turn carried you both? Upon which heavenly gold of the afternoon did you two join, girl and bird, your melancholy flights? What radiant and dreamy sunset gathered you both within its crystalline depth? On what summer afternoon all golden and pink with sweet, blond and joyful sun?

I know well that heaven has rivers of silver and forests of gold; that the heaven of children must have dogs, butterflies, and birds. So, upon which rosebush with roses of eternal harmony, upon which field of emerald and dew will you both

4

be, in your radiant nakedness of golden feathers and pink flesh, you little girl laughing, and you little bird flying and singing in an eternal, fresh and unending idyll?

4.

In the girls' bedroom there is an empty place tonight; I say empty though her mother is sitting in it and no one can remove her from it. But a little bed is missing.

The two sisters, as they were ready to go to bed, all white, pink with life and blonde and warm from the fireplace, ask me, their eyes wide open with sadness and guessing:

"The little girl, where does she sleep tonight?"

"In the children's heaven," I answer as I bite my lips to keep myself from crying.

God, how cold will this night be in heaven!

5.

The little girl died in the afternoon. The following day, with the house already empty of the funeral and angelic pomp, the other sisters would talk, in their playroom, among broken dolls, sewing kits, balls, hanging clothes. On that day they did not go to school. At times they would move around, all excited, forgetful of everything. At times they would sit down, very serious, not knowing exactly why they were crying . . . I had taken them the previous afternoon to the cradle of the suffering girl to say goodbye to her forever. . . . Suddenly:

Lola: "I have a memento of Maria Pepa which none of you has. Look at it. This cross, she gave it to me and I shall never remove it. . ."

Victoria: "But I also have one, no one else has. A bite she gave me in the arm, that made me bleed much. . ."

Lola (her eyes like fists): "I wish she would have given me an even bigger bite than that. . ."

6.

Her sisters have arrived, a circle of whiteness, freshness and joy. They have filled the house and the garden with their laughter, their games, and with the silvery music of their voices. But . . . from within those voices it sounds at times like the sound of her voice, younger, more girlish, less formed, more ethereal, more innocent, more pure. Her accent is among those of her sisters, and now rotting in the tomb, the accent of her voice brings her to life. She is like a girl of crystal and shadow playing with other girls. . .

I did not come out to meet them. I make myself believe that the dead girl is here with her sisters, that she runs, she sings, she laughs, that she—all alone!—fills the house, the garden, all of life.

The sun sets . . . on the porch, pink with sunset, the girls stumble in confusion, between shadows and light yellow from the inside, with their white dresses and their watery voices. A deep sadness, large and humid, like the road leading to the new cemetery rises in me and then leaves among our trees by the road in the cold of the autumn night under the pink clouds now turning mauve. . . . Afternoon sun almost white now abandoning my room, you remind me of her agony. . . . The sun was waving in an endless goodbye; the shadows ended up winning. . . . The mother was sobbing: "How sad you leave, my daughter!"

Like you, sun almost white, she kept losing her color . . . I did not dare kiss her for fear of breaking the life she still had. . .

Cold in the head of the dead girl! Cold in the wall without sun! Cold, like you, wall without sun, was her shaven and dead head. . . . Earlier it had snowed and it never felt to me as cold.

Like you, wall without sun, she kept losing her color. Suddenly, when she died, how cold!

Her little head lay mauve and bent, like a large, dead rose.

7.

God, two things made me always doubt you; one black, the other white: that monstrous creatures be born, and that children die.

Children die! Man is able to bear, with his thought, pain and suffering, but a sick child is only pain, all pain, a white wound without boundaries.

II

Valusia and Marilín

1.

A Little Girl's Portrait

"Will you give me a kiss, Valusia?"

"See if I know how."

Then she runs among the geraniums before I can come close,
like a little bitch, playfully pretending to fall down, flirtatious
and soft, held up by the intense blackness of her direct and
shining tiny eyes. She holds all the joy of all the ignorance
contained in her brief flesh.

"When you become fifteen," I said laughing, "you are
going to be a bundle of trouble, Valusia."

She laughs, madly, throwing back her head, her eyes
never leaving mine, wasting unknowingly all the energy of her
tender, healthy and free five years. At this point, her forehead
clear, her hair cascading backwards, she looks like a woman.

Later on, in a kind of advanced vengeance, she peeks an
eye through every difficult hole: through the wheel of a tiny
cart, through the slats of a chair, through a funnel, through the
leaves of a rose bush, from behind her mother, until little by
little she moves on to something else.

Beautiful, joyful and spontaneous Valusia! God grant that
you stay like this forever and may you find noble souls that do

not rob you of all your joy and leave you only your pain, as so often happens!

She understands the murmur of words I send in the sad look I giver her and pretends to get angry and says, as she beats me:

"Juan Ramón, I do not believe you. . . ." Then she extends her little mouth, pink and fresh, for me to kiss it.

2.

Marilín and the Butterfly

Marilín Santullano, the Polish girl from Asturias, is, as always, looking around, searching (her green eyes wide open against the ground, her little, thick, red hands eager, absentmindedly sniffling); she is always searching on the ground for little pieces of glass, little insects, sticks, whatever; then at last she finds a white butterfly, half dead, at the foot of a poplar tree. She picks it up, cleaning on her apron the dust of her hand with the virgin delicacy that "wants" to be delicate; running, she places it upon a daisy.

"There, so she may die happy."

With her hands behind her back, her fingers nervously crossed, her little stomach protruding, her head fallen to one side, she searches with her marine eyes my eyes, convinced, not knowing why, that she has performed a great deed, deserving that the distant Don Francisco should become suddenly present to her.

Some time later, both of us oblivious for a moment of the butterfly, we find out that the butterfly is no longer on the daisy. Did a bird eat it? Had it revived by the impulse of the flower moved by the breeze? Did the air, or a nearby draft, take it away? Or had it just evaporated, simply as does the dew, in a miraculous assumption, from the soul of the flower to the radiant sky of spring?

Marilín, her shadow lengthened against the hill by the low sun (lavender and green field surrounded by a lavender fence), keeps looking at me in surprise, telling me with her nervous hand what she is unable to and cannot say with her mouth. Her explanation, not being anything, is more accurate, and because it is nothing, it convinces her and me.

3.

Guadarrama, the Sky River

The smaller tower of the Prosperidad, so much in ruins, and the tiny and gray wintery poplars of the Canalillo are sketched today against a dirty sky, lightly marked with green stripes, watery backdrop of the Guadarrama river.

Marilín Santullano suddenly drags her little sister, Valusia, to a window and for a moment, propping her against it, says to her:

"Look, today there are no mountains, there is no Sierra. The thieves took her away last night."

Valusia raises her fine black eyes towards mine, opens her arms, cushioned with three layers of sleeves that have climbed up to suffocate her, and finally throws herself upon me, crying full of distress as if something terrible had happened.

"Today there is no Sierra, Juan Ramón, today there is no Sierra."

4.

The New Tiny Orchard

Has the joyful hour arrived within the rhythm of my heart? I did not want to find out any more. What peace, in the clear March afternoon, with all the windows, the song of birds, the lilacs and almond trees blooming! It felt as if a river of sweet clarity were taking me with certainty to the ideal.

In my exuberance I turned to the little girls. Valusia was hugging one of my legs and Marilín the other. Then I proposed to them to plant an orchard. They went crazy; they kept jumping and saying words that made no sense. First I dug the earth; then I planted on the shores eucalyptus trees and cypresses. Then we buried the seed in little squares for beans, lentils, turnips and oranges . . . we even planted chocolate and noodles. Then we watered everything as the clear sunset was already covering the earth.

What peace and joy! Sweet, vibrant bells sang in the open sunset. Every turn of the breeze let out a new scent, which would then get lost very deep in the soul. The Guadarrama river was disappearing in its strong purity. The memory was peaceful and pain was quiet. Then the sun finally set. The girls, naturally changeable, left.

I stayed by myself, in the tiny orchard, among shadows. The orchard also turned solitary and cold.

III

The Tiny Ray of Sun

    The tiny baby has been awakened in the cradle by a tiny ray of sun entering the dark summer room through a crack in the closed window.

    If the child had awakened without that sun, he would have broken into tears, crying for his mother. But the shining beauty of the tiny ray has opened in his very eyes a magic and flowery garden that holds him bewitched.

    The little child claps hands, laughs and holds long conversations with himself without words, clasping his two feet with his two hands, rocking in his delight.

    He extends his tiny hand to the ray of sun; then his foot (with how much difficulty and patience!); then his mouth; then one eye and he is dazzled; he then laughs while rubbing his closed eye, filling his tight mouth with saliva. If in his fight to play with the ray of sun he hits himself against the railing, he holds his pain and his tears, only that as he laughs his tears break down the beautiful ray of sun into complex and precious rainbows.

    The moment passes and the tiny ray of sun leaves the child, moving little by little, up the wall. The child still follows it with his eyes, mesmerized as if following an impossible butterfly, one real to him.

    Suddenly the sun is gone. In the dark room the child— what is the matter with this child, they all say as they run, what is the matter?

—cries desperately for his mother.

IV

La Vida

All the children had their eyes closed, deeply asleep. I crossed the bedroom slowly—it was a long and narrow room full of windows resembling a train at dawn—looking at each one of them, round, rosy, smiling, peaceful.

Suddenly two large magnetic and fluttering eyes were staring at me, shining, fixed, like black burning coals. They belonged to a child lying down and quiet like the others but not sleeping.

Oh, those eyes open and mute, alone in the long room where all other eyes were closed! Those eyes, no doubt, were open long before I was able to see them; they were eyes fixed upon themselves, with no relation to others, dreaming with their own conscience and without noise, following visions without reins; eyes that will stay open, no doubt, after I pass by and, for how long?

That child, awake in the midst of all the other sleeping children did not look to me to be the only life in that train that rode in the sleep of life, but rather the one and only true death.

V

Jeranita

(Moguer)

The poor boy was called Jeranita. His taste was only for things of church and skirts. At dusk he organized, with other children of his street, tiny processions with candles and songs; he danced alone in the vestibule of his home "sevillanas" with castanettes and high kicks in the air. He ran around crazily with the girls, skipped rope with more delicate moves than theirs and sighed and made points with semantic diminutives.

His mother, a kind of police guard dressed in mourning, broad and with a greying mustache, opened wide the door of the vestibule, that the boy and the girls had half closed, and chased him with a stick. The boy slipped away out of her hands like a flower and faced her from the street, teasing her with frog leaps and erratic jumps.

The mother shouted at him, beside herself, howling: "Lazy bum, always hungry for good food but always from the mackerel to the sardine, from the sardine to the mackerel!"

Jeranita, as if all this were a game, skipped down the street braiding his hop and skip like girls do, repeating to himself the refrain: "From the mackerel to the sardine, from the sardine to the mackerel!"

VI

Cold

The father wears a warm coat, a thick scarf. He also wears a flat face, very red. He looks well fed, his eyes are bloodshot and he smokes a cigar. The child wears light clothes, summer clothes, his visible flesh everywhere blue.

The boy—like a girl, a flower—complains: ''I feel so cold, daddy!''

The father pays him little heed.

''Men feel no cold.''

''When you were a child,'' answers the son, ''you must have felt cold, daddy!''

The father: ''Sometimes.''

He then puffs deeply on his cigar and belches ham and sausage.

The child: ''Yes, I also feel it many times; only sometimes I say it; others I don't.''

VII

The Disagreeable Child

    The poor child did not know it, nor did his mother. He had a tiny face like an old man, disagreeable gestures, irritating voice. But since children have never seen themselves from the outside, he used to focus with his inside on the pleasant outside of others.

    His every gesture was awkward: trying to pet the dog, or play, or sing, or laugh. Only when, in a moment of unconscious divination, he would break down crying would he then move others to charity and love.

    The rest of the family tried to overcompensate by giving the mother false assurances, but she would water them down, suddenly red from a constant pain. Whatever the child would eat, drink, or ask, even when asking for nothing important, would cause annoyance. When the poor child would finally leave, always with a face serious from the many recriminations given him by false love, he would carry always a simple smile, truly distant, which to everyone else seemed very sad.

VIII

"Maricón!"

He wanted to buy, like his rich friends, an elegant Panama hat. His uncle brought one for him from Huelva on a May afternoon on the five o'clock coach; an afternoon that became for him the vestibule of paradise.

The hat arrived at the street of Los Molinos wrapped in delicate silk paper.

He put on the hat and stood in front of the door to his house:

"Maricón!"

He would then smuggle the hat under his shirt and run with it, hidden, halfway up the street of Azana, where the houses of the rich began. There he would put on the hat. Someone from his own street, going in the opposite direction, would spot him: "Maricón!"

IX

The Bird Cage of the Children

Under the sun of an April morning, in an ugly apartment house across the street, with evil monsters in the cornices, the children that live on the highest floor are looking out—for what?—behind the balcony's wire cage.

Their mother, no doubt, is unable to take them to freer suns and so she sets them there, like little birds, so that they may breathe the good of the new blue day.

Seeing them reminds me of a school without walls that a tribe from Aschantis, which visited us years ago, used to set in the midst of their buildings, and where black children would spend their time chanting the lessons of their books.

These other birds, blond and pink, entertain themselves by talking to the parrot about the evil-tempered Puerto Rican woman from a few floors below, or by repeating to him the chant of the carrot vendor, of the asparagus vendor, the orange vendor, or by begging for more from the blind man with the dark glasses and the clarinet, or talking about the silly woman with the castanettes.

They distract me, but I do not mind. I would willingly give up half an hour of singing lessons with the Cuban woman from the floor above in exchange for a whole day of twitters and laughter under the April sun. Yes, their joy, sad to me, induces me to work, to put more wings in all I do, to dream of a way really to grow wings and fly away from these balconies, to go away and return to our rested mothers bringing in our mouths new flowers and pure water.

X

Olympia

(Portrait of a Girl)

She looks like a doll that has just been removed from its box: straight lines, colors that look alive—rouge, very black large eyes, generously dressed in blue. She comes to eat lunch with us and then she leaves for school. I follow her on the road, coming and going, her face always serious. She appears as if she were always ready, with no hesitation, never joyful yet always joyful, as she looks at the violets.

XI

The Royal Cricket

What anguish that cricket brought me in that strange month of June (concave and deep June). It sat there on my open windowsill but it sounded deep within my own loneliness, like a huge bell, in the very inner center of my ear! My sleep turned into an infinite shock and nightmare; the whole summer sky turned black, transformed into a monotonous, heavy and sonorous drip of molten stars and eternal shadows; the immense sea, Nubian black, became condensed into a brief wave, terrible and suffocating, which choked me with every rhythmic blow, as if the whole world, in concentrated form, leaned upon my auditive brain, while I became its prisoner by the head (what pulls!).

Finally I could stand it no more. I asked Honorito Igelmo, the caretaker's son and owner of the royal cricket, if he would sell it to me. I offered him fifty cents, one dollar, five, as much as he wanted. I planned to take that dark animal of steel to the Retiro Park and make him a permanent guest of the most distant grass.

The child opened his eyes widely, in astonishment; they looked to me like two huge melancholic crickets, carrying deep, sad music, which because of my proposition, I thought, had turned to pain.

Thanks to the living god of silence, alive for my sake that day, that was not the case! The young Castillian answered:

"For fifty cents I will bring you, sir, five crickets that can really sing!"

XII

The Young Beggar

It is winter. Mercedita Saro is already standing by the corner, wrapped in her pointed shawl—only one-fourth of one, as she has cut it from a woman's shawl—covering with it her mouth. She looks cute as a button. Her small round head, her hair combed back (with so much care. Whose?), and her stiff pigtail braided at the back with a white ribbon in the end reminds me of the full moon with a star nearby (which in turn reminds me of a night buoy with a lantern at the farthest end. What mysteries hide in little things!).

She knows me already and her tiny fresh eyes, joyfully sad, see me coming and smile at me from all the corners of these streets. Instead of giving her money, which I am supposed to drop in the nicotine-smeared hat of the drunk man at the corner, I take her to a bakery or a candy store and buy her whatever she likes; she comes along with me as if on a stroll, telling me her things until she eats up all of whatever she might have wished.

I believe she feels protected by me. She figures out, confusedly no doubt, that her father at the corner is a man with many rights. She has heard so much about him here and there but she has not been able to make sense of it or put it together. He is The Man from Lista, Rachavol, The Executioner, someone strange and tragic, notorious in the dusk of dawn and evening of those cobwebbed, low streets with nakedness and dirty faces. As she comes near him, the young girl tells me, pretending while pressing against my coat:

"Sir, be very careful. This is my father and he does not like for me to eat sweets."

XIII

The Newspaper Man

He is so tiny he can hardly be seen at night in the ill-lighted street. He jumps upon one from everywhere, almost from within oneself. He nails under my arm a newspaper larger than he. With the paper already under my arm, his hands in the deep pockets of a huge coat belonging to someone else, he shouts in musical cadences:

"The *Corres* with the death of Gallitoooo!"

"Child," reprimands his sister, a bit older than he, as she opens the tiny window of her little home, lighted and warm in the kiosk, "this is not true; the bullfighter died four days ago!"

He walks straight, on his toes, toward her:

"So? I know that. Four days ago; but I sell newspapers, silly!"

He turns around with a painful bullfighting walk—also military around his tiny possessions and poverty—and looking at the shadow a gas lantern casts beside him (lemon green in the copper thickness of a dead and dwarf tree that harbors the half moon) he talks to himself, being the only one listening:

"I am really something!"

XIV

The Clown

    We moved you about, here and there, like a suitcase, a basket. And since you were a suitcase and a basket that moved and annoyed more than the other forty-four pieces of luggage, we were always shouting at you and reprimanding you. You were always left without us in hotel rooms. We used to leave you on a bed with baby sitters, your affections towards us lost on them. You had the flu in Mexico, the scarlet fever in Barcelona, also in Lisbon; until one day in Madrid you had had enough and refused to travel any more.

    They took you away in a white limousine, on a carnival afternoon, amidst confusing sounds, shouts, car wheels, horns, and shoving at the door of the hotel from people who wanted nothing to do with you. You were taken in the opposite direction of all other cars, through streets with closed shops that not even you knew, as the afternoon was starting to clean itself, up there, turning pink and other colors not proper for an infant but more suitable for young adults.

    Now we come and go without you. We carry no basket with us nor suitcase belonging to you. We see the smiling spring in Paris, autumn in Lisbon, winter in Barcelona. We carry no live luggage to leave in hotel rooms or to reprimand on the trains. You must have become accustomed to a cricket or a mallow; your living heart is dry now, though it beat so much and so uselessly for us.

XV

The Young Banana Vendor

"All for a dollar. They come from Havana; come from Havana!"

The girl moves about fast—all red within her black hood, with a basket full of yellow bananas, that look more yellow in the gray day—splashing in the rain, which bends her over the shining sidewalk and wraps her up as within a funnel of sadness. Her voice sounds more melodious through the rain—at times lost, at other times as sharp as a nail.

"All for a dollar. They come from Havana; come from Havana!"

The street is deserted. The sky leans on the street as a thick and suffocating partition. The young girl, like a tiny fish, moves about without any sense of father or mother through Havana!"

XVI

A Boy's Portrait

(Miguel German)

"How beautiful these stones in your street! They are much more beautiful than the stones in my street. . . . These ants in your garden, how beautiful they are! They are more beautiful than the ones in my garden. . . . And those branches, those bricks, the little birds, the caretaker . . . how, how, how!"

He finds that everything is better than that which he has. He is tall, obedient and enthusiastic; he has a charming immature beauty that is noble and open, with the softness of his mother and the strength, still tender, of his father; he is as healthy as both of them. His father complains, at times, that he feels sorry for him in life, because he is so good and transparent.

Now he is beginning to grow and his spreading thoughts cast no shadows on his nobility. His eyes, now set within his adolescent spring, open as they gaze at sweet flowers with bright light. There is nothing to fear, father! He carries as a shield on this earth where we are now loose, a double sun for the two hemispheres of life: intelligence, of all the least useful, and heart, of all the least useless.

XVII

The Forgotten Canary

(Madrid)

Every afternoon, the children from across the street bring out to the sun—this feeble, high sun on the somber street—a baby canary. The children join the canary with imprisoned wings in the larger cage of the wired balcony that imprisons their feet. All together shout, sing to one another, clap hands, imitate one another, pretend to fly, and laugh.

Then slowly, without my noticing it, silence begins to fall. I continue my work, my dreams, imprisoned in body and soul, and I am not able to tell if the children and the bird are silent or if I keep hearing them in dreams. The hours of free light move on and the imprisoned light must be turned on.

Suddenly, on seeing the balcony without children, I hear the silence. Then I do not dream I hear or do not hear I dream. In the absolute silence of the moment everything is closed, a mute clamor, the size of the birds' sky, rises within me, a sky of flight; this is because the baby canary is left alone every afternoon, all silent, as if it were not outside in the closed balcony, in the high cold which—for a bird—is as large as the size of the world.

XVIII

Rafael Vázquez

His mother is telling me. He is there, listening to it absorbed, when I am not looking. All of his fine and delicate life climbs to his blue eyes like the stem of a young rush that was opening on high, in its eagerness, two flowers. When I look at him he leans his blond head toward his heart, as toward a nest.

They live in the Avenue near the bullfighting ring which he hates, being so sentimental and filled with light. His mother says that he says:

"Next Sunday when the bullfighters, picadors and people come to the bullring I am going to stand in the middle of the street with my arms opened, telling them: 'Go home, go home; there is no bullring! There is no bullring! I have pulled it down. I am an architect and I have built in its place houses for working people.'"

He follows, absorbed, the narration of his mother with a living fire, yearning and perfumed, in his eyes; the rest of this slender and graceful flower seems to be emptied of life. Then, as I look at him and caress his hair he leans his head toward his heart, as toward a nest.

XIX

"Little Violet"

They brought us, as a present, a white pigeon "for us to eat." After seeing and petting it, who could eat it? We gave it away to the two children of the gardener to take care of.

"What will you do with it?"

Maria, the oldest one, "Little Violet" as we used to call her, grayish and cute, with green eyes, her hair grayish-brown with oil, her teeth yellow, immediately jumped:

"We'll take care of it, sir!"

Their father killed the pigeon that same afternoon and the whole family ate it; that is, the father and the boy, Faneguillas, who was the father's favorite child. The mother and the girl were happy smelling it, forced to appear nice.

Next day, when I came to the house, the children were sitting at the door playing with pins:

"How is the pigeon?" I asked anxiously.

The boy stood up, stuck out his tummy and rubbed it in circles:

"It is here, well taken care of."

"Little Violet," Maria, imitated her brother, smiling sadly:

"Here, sir, well taken care of."

(1908)

XX

Manolillo

In the solitude of the distant mountain where that
morning he had been left alone with his donkey, it being a
holiday, Manolillo wanted to celebrate Christmas Eve with her.
He painted his face coal black and ocher red; he also painted a
moustache, his eyebrows, and crosses on his forehead and his
cheeks. Then he proceeded to paint the donkey's forehead and
ears. Then he sang and jumped around the donkey, for he
realized something was the matter with her as she was sad on
that short and cold afternoon.

He came to realize, at times, that he was not having a
good time and felt like crying. As the sun set, the dusk of the
sea turned black and red like his face. Aware, then, of his pain,
he was about to throw himself on the ground when the donkey
bent one of her back legs, then the other, and remained thus
squatting for a while. Then she lay down looking sad.

Manolillo forgot himself and ran to her, eager and
astonished. He understood vaguely that something was wrong,
that the donkey, perhaps, might die.

The night had completely arrived. Since he could not
carry the donkey to his hut, and it being very cold, the boy
searched the mountains in the dark, gathering twigs and
branches; he piled them next to the donkey and lit a large
candle that swelled the donkey's strange head and his own,
painted red and black, which he had forgotten. He then
proceeded to console the donkey and lay on top of her as he
remembered some half-forgotten story of a mule warning with
her breath, on a cold night like this one, a little boy born in a
manger.

This time, however, it was the other way around, and he was feeble and small.

(1913)

XXI

The Clearing

The little child has been sitting—for how long?—in the humid, hard sand, waiting, I know not for whom, who had left him there without help—could it be that woman, the one with the white shawl with brown squares, half hidden behind the clearing with the police guard? Since the woman and the guard are not with the child, he and a large moon are all that are left in the large esplanade. The moon is rising, opaque and cold—October—dazed by the dusk, from behind the tower of the Guindalera.

The child, for a moment, in a fickleness of his eyes, sees the moon—moon, moonlight, moonsong—and throwing his head back he extends, as far as he can, his arms toward her. Then, his tiredness and forgetfulness coming together, he stares at a tiny bug crawling by; then he listens to a trumpet, its out-of-tune sound sadly wounding the sunset with dramatic bands, or entertains himself by running his finger around a tiny puddle of water, which, like a dripping faucet, he has formed under his seat.

He cries a little, but he soon forgets and tires of crying; then again his eyes become lost up high and he extends again his arms, in a tiny, immense and desperate effort toward the moon; she looks now clear and shining, moving the night over the high solitude.
(1916)

XXII

Leontine

1.

Leontine has come to Sevilla, sweet and firm, on the white steamer Manuel Arnús by the flaming Guadalquivir river.

When she wants to be sweet she makes herself almost invisible; when hard, she becomes steel. Her sweetness is difficult and her pride easy.

She walks ahead and alone looking for flowers, birds, old people, the highest and deepest spots, searching for the secret which best fits her delicate and proud soul.

She is made of beginnings and ends; one day, with eyebrows opened she looks like a baby; another, her eyebrows straight, she looks like an old woman. She laughs and cries as if, at times, she understood. She is a thirteen-year-old female secret. She has the seed of all the virtues and the root of all inequity.

2.

Leontine and God Father

God Father was riding a thick cloud, directing a storm
over Spain. He liked to alternate, with the art of a millenial
critic, the rich and treasured variations of his central
pyrotechnics and thus wanted to repeat an old lighting from
the time of Paradise. But as he is so old with eternal old age, he
lost his footing on the cloud and fell down upon the Segovian
mountain.

The storm, without a conductor, did not know what to do
and proceeded to divide itself up into separate accumulations,
gathering its failure whenever it could. Clouds and mountains
remained then fixed, similar to one another as touching
neighboring kingdoms. Here and there, through the cracks in
the central casting of the heavenly decoration, a green sun
came out, lighting up all that had become wet, in a strident
sound of color.

Leontine, my American niece—almost fourteen—looking
heavenly white and heavenly blue, was walking the high fields,
all absorbed, gathering autumn crocuses. She caught with her
side view God Father falling down and in one impulse of ideal
energy she moved towards him, jumping. She remembered
him from the pictures in my books, just as she saw him: the
head in triangular shape, an eye in the middle, cascading white
beard and his hands pointing down.

Leontine, perhaps, believes in no god whatsoever, but,
perhaps she feels respect for the possible mystery. She
brought close to God Father her delicate, pale sweetness, and
spoke to him, almost with her thoughts: "Poor God Father!"
Then she replaced on his hands the globe of the world and
looked around for a possible solution. She took advantage of a
violent cloud that was passing very low; she pushed God
Father softly and set him back on his place.

She watched him go up into space. Her eyes and lips made parallel lines, yet smiled from a corner while her brain kept sending hand-blown kisses. She then returned, jumping, brushing the hay from her hair, a bit more serious, to her dripping crocuses.
(1929)

XXIII

"The Bad Poet"

(Río Piedras)

In the deep, triangular shade of the little door, which half buried us within a well of air becoming fuller with the fog of that rainy afternoon, and sitting between the heavenly thin singer and the black girl—all bony and stooped, whose shy words sounded as if coming from outside of her—the "bad poet," like a joyful and strong animal, was shyly reaching for my hand.

His own hand was short, thick as if cut to measure to his narrow, wrinkled forehead where his hair formed an isle as if it grew out of the back of his head. That whole bulk of flesh fifteen years old, that whole being of flat flesh whose main spring seemed to hide in his raised nose, appeared to be upside down, disturbed, mistaken and confused. If on account of some verbal exchange his mouth laughed, it would do so by shrinking into a wrinkle all of his life; then a new face would appear hinting to some other human possibilities.

I looked at him with anguished respect. The heavenly singer, all thin and gray: face, hair, song (like mauve steel), had just finished singing Schubert's *Serenade* (his clouds with moonlight made the black girl hide her eyes behind the back of a chair, and they also left soft, white shadows of angels and virgins upon the raised face of the "bad poet") and the time had come for him to enter the show with hard, square realism. He seemed full of confidence within his secret. He declaimed with gestures and bodily ornaments:

36

Your voice sounds happy in my ear,
like the enchanting breath of Aeolus,
when, the Myriad Star asleep in fear,
through the palm trees moves quietly,
Sweet teacher . . .

Everytime that he, in verse or prose, referred to the
"sweet voice of his teacher," his face became transformed,
shaking in a terrible way, as if he were coming out from the
underground into the most divine light of the sun, in a
frightening resurrection of all that is dead. He then took on a
fierce expression, like that of a criminal against destiny,
against himself or against God.

There was no room in him for doubt, his laughter was self-
confident, the master of everything he was not aware of. He
continued:

Sweet teacher,
Do not abandon me in one only sense
for I am lacking in only one . . .

When he finished, after a moment of hesitant
accommodation, as if he had been left in a place not his own or
had decided to join us for a while, he hurled insults at himself.
He called himself "unwary," "bucolic," "bad poet," while
smiling his antediluvian smile.

He returned to his chair and sat there stiff, his square
hands on his thighs, his face lifted towards some unknown
clearing, shining on him, from above, true light. I then spoke to
him humbly, as to a superior, about his poem. I said that the
last two verses belonged to a great poet and that a man able to
express his feelings as he had done should consider himself
fortunate. He, however, was still listening to himself in the
place on stage where he was earlier, repeating softly some
words which seemed reluctant to leave his mouth (sweet metal
on a magnet) tasting them in the distance, as if his internal
eyes were touching an exquisite, tall rose.

Sweet teacher . . . in one sense . . .

In the white, crude cavities of his eyes, stomped, deserted as a beach by the moon, the signs of love and pain disguised as brutal joy, and as they rose and grew they mixed and outlined a vision; then, two precious stones, hard and fine, formed in the exact place of his heroic and pure eyes, which he no doubt owned in the depths of his seed.

(1936?)

XXIV

Max, the Blue Child

(Caribbean Sea)

Max came out on deck wearing patent leather shoes, a white, loose collar, a hand-embroidered tie, a new suit, a checkered cap; all this had been bought unseen by him or the buyer. He turned his blue face toward me and winked a quick gesture, smiling all over. His smile seemed misty to me. I looked closer. I saw a cloud, which I had not noticed before, in one eye. His face was also covered with powder.

(All through the journey from Santo Domingo to Cuba, Max walked around almost naked, without shoes, for they hurt him unless he powdered his feet. Max had been taken from the fields of Puerto Plata and was being shipped to Santiago, the city itself, to live with I know not which brothers he had never met and about whom he talked to me, hesitant and doubtful. An insensitive Haitian, educated in France, had taken over the ship and treated Max, in an effort to be funny, like a little dog. The child followed him submissively, though he despised him. Max liked most to be alone, as if fleeing. I remember his eager chest, very bony and throbbing high, leaning out over the railing. I remember his face against the low moon of Haiti while the unending ship lay anchor near Jacmel, Jeremie and Les Cayes. I remember him when a musical instrument would sound on the bow of the ship and Max would go into a rapture glued to the musical air, striving to enter almost within the instrument itself.)

It made me sad to see his face covered with powder. He resembled a humble little clown. I invited him to drink with me some juice so that he could talk better. I said: "Come Max, why did you put powder on your face?"

He answered with simple shame, his diverging eye going very stray, its white cloud thick, the voice difficult: "To look whiter at dinner tonight." Then he added hesitatingly: "And to look whiter to my brothers."

"Whiter? And why do you wish to be whiter? Black and white are the same, two colors, one is as good as the other. Look at it this way, Max. There is white marble and black marble, black eyes and clear eyes, white doves and dark doves. Don't you see the violets? Some are white, some mauve. The moon—look at it—it is black and white at the same time. Black and white are into everything in the world which is also black and white. There are also other colors, sharp and somber, sweet and sour: yellow, blue, red, and all are beautiful colors; and there are people of all colors. Do you think a white horse is more beautiful than a black one, that a black wave is more evil than a white wave? Don't you like the sea at night? White violets or mauve violets are the same. I prefer the mauve over the white."

Max stood on his toes as if he felt taller and removed with a rough and vibrant hand the powder from his face. He then looked at me happy, smiled straight, for he always smiled sideways, and said, clean, firm and tender as he was leaving: "That's right. Thank you."
(1936)

XXV

Francisco González Aramburu

(Spanish Child in Mexico)

He answered me softly, his voice almost brushing me, straight and delicate, his eyes on mine, with the exact touch of a sensitive blade: "Yes."

I had asked him: "Are you the poet?" I, then, asked him if he had written anything while at sea. He answered quickly with a short "Yes" and with emotion, his voice turned inward, he added: "The Tempest in the Tropics." There were verses there I do not forget:

"and again that slate blue returns . . ."

I continued asking him things of interest to both of us and he would answer brief and sure. He spent long times by my side, walking slowly and pressing one of my fingers with his hand. He looked drawn, withdrawn into a world that was within him, which the external visible, the general external, could not understand. He had been chosen to read the greeting of the Spanish children to President Martí, which he never read, though I am sure that he, made of feeling, did not care for the show.

We had to return to shore and leave the Spanish children in Mexico. He asked me, as I was hugging him: "Will you remember me?" He then gave me a small red book. It was an edition of *Platero and I* which had come out in July in Madrid and I had seen to the finish. He had written inside, in a firm hand, this dedication: "Juan Ramón: In the name of the Spanish children going to Mexico, we greet you and dedicate to you your book, for it has amused us and taught us so much. Francisco González Aramburu."

The ship crossed in front of Vedado at two in the afternoon accompanied by a crazy, eager, melancholic salute of horns. Hundreds of cars ran parallel to it by the Malecon. The children were huddled together at the stern as if forming one single being, one flesh and one soul, the one new life of Spain. Amongst them, appearing very clear to me, in the invisible distance, was Francisco González Aramburu, exemplar of Spanish children "whom I will always remember.

Moral beauty, which appears always great in the child or the grown-up, how those who accommodate, the selfish, flee you, change you, lose you!
(Havana 1937)

Part II

Compassionate Shoulder

(Friendly Hand)

I

Drunk

(The First Time)

He came in stumbling, his face bloated, all red up to the top of his forehead, carrying a very sad joy which appeared to be a previous sadness rejoiced, trying to force his face into a smile under the sadness in his swollen eyes, a sadness which the alert conscience did not abandon in the unconscious.

He reached a chair where his indignant mother could see him come in, and managed to say:

"I made peace with Pepe."

The mother's indignation did not know how to come out, if as crying or laughing; she laughed unwillingly, just a little as she got up, then she ran to hide her crying, this time willingly.

The son ended up falling on the made bed, senseless, congested, breathing with difficulty, in a sleep without flying dreams, so deep that it could only be separated from death because the air kept coming in and out of his body, a body uninhabited by sensation, like an empty house.

He had never drunk before. The demands of life, the need to give in in order to coerce, the miseries of living in a nearly savage village in Spain forced him to fall down this once. He slept very deeply, as if in his last shame, his true self; he slept as if he had been already assassinated and left out in the cold or as if a virtuous woman, forced naked, had left her defenseless nakedness, dead.

He woke up serene and completely in control of himself. He became sad later. He smiled without any joy with a smile outside of himself, added to his mouth as if painted. He approached his mother, put his arm around her shoulder for a moment, hugged her deeply, picked up his hat and left for the street.

II

Madrid's Blind

They are returning from the concert, hurriedly, all smiles, playful, daring, through the cold night, under the autumn branches turned to sharp gold by the magic of the neon lights that illumine them, and (higher up) under the green, liquid stars, black, closed in, black, black.

"How divine Mendelssohn! You don't have to tell me! That is music!"

Whoever spoke whistles while twisting his body in a romantic contortion, as if fully pregnant with heavenly elixer, his distorted white face full like a moon in the cold of the great shadow.

"But, then, what about Schubert?" another voice sings, facing the first speaker and hanging on to his lapels in such a way that both faces face together the zenith. "Oh, Schubert, Schubert of my life!"

Then he shows the white of his eyes to the sky.

They all move playfully as laughing mutes, now drunk with a dated sentimentalism of waltzes and barcaroles, music at its purest for them, a flock without freedom, their life at a standstill; this is the elegance, the delicacy (the feminine word here makes one also cry) of their poor souls, of their confined woman.

Suddenly, in their drunken and fast march, those ahead realize no other familiar footsteps follow them . . .

"Paco!"

"Paco!"

"Paco!"

They pretend to be looking here and there, their eyes still high. Paco does not answer. Only silence, dark and cold.

They come together melancholically and stand still, silent, their heads down, their blind eyes now touching the ground, afraid to get lost, just like sheep, black, black, black.

III

Cruel Ruins

(Compassion)

> "Birds . . .! Little birdsss!"
> A saleswoman

Thus the sales pitch. It snows. And it seems as if the little birds that woman sells have just now died of cold; and one loses one's appetite to eat even greens.

"Birds, little birdsss!" How much cruelty in the sales pitch! It sounds like an effort to tenderize the little birds for cruel teeth. It seems to say: "Come to them without fear, the poor things, the defenseless ones, the innocent ones, for they are already dead . . .!" But instead of causing the contrary effect people buy them with smiles.

Snow. Madrid turns black and white, its roofs change into skies and the façades into foundations. One would expect, when the thaw comes, to see one single steppe, like a huge, blank book, left open. One single sparrow, wet and wilted, darker and looking more like the color of straw in the day, flies awkwardly from the low balcony of a dark and uninhabited house, to the street; alone, now distant, the sales pitch: "Birds, little birdsss!" flies by like a sad flock towards nothingness.

IV

The Sister

(Madrid)

I stopped him in the Avenue. He was walking fast by the pure, morning garden, crying, dirty and feeling miserable. His face, filthy and young, almost adolescent, was slipping away under the tears—darkness, sickness, wine, misery.

The pain bent him over. He could hardly stand on his feet. While carrying on a halting conversation his body took him from one side to another; he would then lean against a tree, or sit on a bench and would not fall to the ground because I was holding him.

He told me everything in his sadness. He was a thief, a drunk, a criminal and everything one can imagine, he said. Now his sister had died.

And he kept on crying all broken up.

His sister dead! In the fresh clarity of the September garden with a touch of autumn, that word sounded like the name of the morning: His sister! How and who had she been, that sister who made this man good?

He had to leave. I accompanied him for a while consoling him. Then I followed him with my eyes till I lost him in the green and blue, that heap of garbage that walked crying.

V

The Angel of Pain

"There should be some compassion," the old woman was telling the poet. Look here, sir. I was once in a museum, contemplating, absorbed in a painting representing *The Angel of Pain*. Suddenly a woman, opulent and disagreeable, dressed luxuriously, and convinced, no doubt, that I was a hindrance in her way, pushed me. 'Pity all that money gone to waste,' I shouted at her, so that she could hear me, 'who could have it to buy *The Angel of Pain*.' Though it is possible that if I had the painting I would not appreciate beauty the way I do."

She then looked at the poet with a smile of mutual understanding.

VI

The Poor Monkey

The spring afternoon had already turned long and at the time of the high sun one could hear in the street the tambourine of the gypsies.

They were an old woman with a face of red ocher, a skirt covered with painted patches of old clothes and a body of flat dirt; a young man, with no other attraction than a sash of a magic and healthy blue, and a naked monkey.

Of the three the only one really working was the monkey, not counting the pounding of the tambourine by the young man and the begging of the old woman. The obedient monkey—he was tied to a chain three times heavier than he—would do everything, but looked so sad!

The sun turning red in a cloud of dust, was sliding, pink, over the cobblestones of the street, accentuating all colors in an excess of light against the background: the sour trees, the green and yellow public buses, and the pants of the military.

They would all file up in front of the monkey: military personnel and priests, ladies and young women, and all would cross smiling at the monkey all tied up and sad.

The gypsies sat by the running water and the monkey sat by them, on a stone. They were eating something; the monkey was looking naked and hungry at the captain in red and blue, with a sword and stars; at the monk with the Cross of Calatrava all red on top of the thickness of his arm holding the cape; at the ladies, with feathers, fox skins and sables around their necks; at the young women with loose blouses, belts and ties of many colors. . . .

From an acacia tree two sparrows were singing at the monkey while the sky was rising fresh and naked.

VII

Candido

The moon was resting over Madrid asleep. She was quiet and green through the copper exhalations of the sharp lights of eleven o'clock. I, called by spring, sat out in the garden to look at the moon.

Dreams came and went, and the hour passed, fast and inadvertently upon my heart, just as the brief low clouds over the moon.

In my ecstasy I came almost to realize I was not alone in the garden; but my eyes would climb back up to the sky and there was no one else in the night but she and I.

A soft touch upon my shoulder brought me out of my ecstasy.

"Sir, are you not feeling well? Sir, would you like me to call Mr. Calandre?"

It was Candido, spying on me, astonished and concerned, unaware that the moon was looking at me from the sky.

"No, man, no. I need nothing."

But he would not leave despite all my requests and I had to abandon the garden in the most beautiful part of the night.

Candido kept insisting:

"If you desire anything . . ."

And he would look at me with that noble, green and stray look that gives him the air of a noble dog, with all its nobility.

VIII

Carnival

    Facing my window, the old paralytic man sits in his gallery, in the sun, his forehead resting against the glass panels, dozing, all sunk to the sour sound of the drum and the flute that three men, dressed in red and black, play by the lonely clearing, now turned to dust in a sickly light green. The old man opens his eyes. Then he goes back to sleep. From his sleep to death there is no more than half a meter of tiredness.

    I, with my suitcases ready, look at the blue sky, where the melodious sounds of the Castellana resound, oblivious to everything. A few white clouds cross the sky, as nowadays trains move on the earth and ships on the sea.

    Down in the garden, oblivious to everything, two masks calmly talk to each other: love and death.

IX

The Young Sparrow

I sat on the bench, under the rich sun smelling of autumn petunias and started to imagine that the reef, passing by, full of blue shadows under the ripe banana trees, was a river. Into the river I threw my thoughts.

Suddenly a bloated young sparrow came jumping little jumps toward me, looking at me with his two tiny eyes of black crystal. He kept coming. I kept calling him as to a little dog, the only call I recalled at the unforeseen moment, and the young sparrow kept coming.

I had nothing to give him. I searched in all my pockets, knowing I had nothing. I searched the surrounding area for something he could catch on with his eyes. Nothing. If he had understood me I would have told him: "Wait, I am going to my house, about a mile from here and I will be back at once." But he did not understand me. And little by little, though I wanted to keep him with me, he left, leaving me with the dying afternoon, sad.

X

Friends?

Those poor women (friends?) would receive in Madrid gallant propositions and in London they would be thrown out of the city: white faces and black hands; dressed, unfortunately, to call attention; their hairdos most alarming; their overcoats serve more as decoration than to protect against the cold; lots of flowers and shamelessness. They believe, in sum, that life is a joke and they spend the day and night sharpening their wits to come up with unfortunate comparisons.

They have been to some cheap musical—the Quinteros —and the most important thing for them is to sharpen the sticks to play billiard balls. And what about style? They dress like Russian soldiers, like police guards, like parrots, and yet they laugh at other women. And culture? A letter, for them, is a cathedral, badly built.

I, watching them strolling on this Sunday afternoon, think of seamstresses, of flowers, of the sky, of trees, in a constant desire for harmony and melody.

XI

The Untimely Sales Pitch

How weird, how terribly strange that sales pitch of the fruit vendor in the night! It was very late, everyone had already had dinner, all the windows were closed to the cold of the changed midseason, and one could hear, behind the wooden blinds, distant and sweet pianos.

And suddenly that shout: "Bananas, good bananas! I am giving them away!"

Was he drunk? A joker? I looked oout. No, it was a seller and he had with him his bananas: "I am giving them away!" And what a powerful voice!

I threw down some coins. I waited. The sales pitch was heard no more. A few footsteps hurriedly became distant, I know not if they were happy footsteps fleeing at last the cold and the untimely hour.

XII

He asked the shoemaker to put taps on his boots. With them on and the spurs he wore that resounded, even though he hardly ever rode a horse (which when he did it made him look the picture of the ridiculous gentleman) he walked the streets pretending somebody was walking on them. Being so short, so dark, and making so much noise, he resembled a beetle. He warned everyone not to step on him; he wore fantastic sunglasses, larger than the orbits of his eyes—eyes made for people that talk, not croak—in order to reduce the size so he could absorb into his eyes the largest part of those people that approached him. He looked around with his head fallen to one side, leaning over his shoulder like a monkey; when he laughed through his cobwebbed, bony face hidden under a confusion of hair, bones and wrinkles, he seemed as if he were about to come completely unglued. Not to mention his shadow! It was a stick with a knot, a scarecrow in winter, a cockroach's skeleton. In spite of all this he was allowed to take people's pulses with those black tweezers of his fingers and even write prescriptions. And how did he manage to procreate? This is not known, but children his wife had and they were healthy, though she was not, a heavy bird from the street. He was junk, a discarded utensil, a broken toy.

60

XIII

Sunday for Two

The young man arrived first, singing, down the street. He was tall, thin, copper colored, his beard and hair unkempt for years, filthy to the point of total confusion. He was singing flamenco tunes. At first no one paid any attention to him, and so he did not make a penny. Then someone who liked what he heard threw some coins to him from a balcony, which made noise on reaching the pavement. The man, encouraged, started to bring out his tunes from far deep within himself and form his own chorus of accompaniment and profile his own dance in an exhibition of filth.

An old man came too, up the street, very small and dried up, smiling, a cigarette butt stuck to his lip, an eye clouded, his back covered with a small blanket with urine on the edges, leaning on a walking stick. On arriving near the singer he stared in ecstasy at his voice and moves. Carried by the enthusiasm of the moment, or so that the singer would not break his song, or for other more selfish reasons, the old man, hat in hand, started to beg around for the singer.

He collected and collected money—the singer would not let him out of his sight—from above, from below, from around, from the balconies and from passing cars. Finally he approached the singer, then ending a string of wailing sounds, and poured in his hands a stream of copper, his face in rapture.

The filthy young man offered him a twisted toast of rotten and absurd grace, and bending his body in a deep bow, his filthy cap in hand, he left, running down the street without giving the old man a nickel. The old man left, walking up the street, sad, still smiling, puffing from his unlit cigarette butt and begging, though now almost not daring to and only from time to time, in the anticipated assurance he would not receive any money for himself, while the moon was already coming out of the night, lonely.

XIV

His Other I

As my friend descended the stairs, and as he reached a certain spot, suddenly I saw in him, the other. It never failed. I do not know if he knew, if he was aware that something more of him was visible, though perhaps he ignored that he carried it with him.

As in a weird, annoying, offensive and ugly separate profile, I could see the other him from above, the door of my apartment still open, saying goodbye.

In no way did it resemble him. It was as if by a sudden sleight of hand he had been replaced by an extrahuman self. It appeared as if made up of the whole of him but without him, or as if he had been deformed, indented, blackened, as if passed through a sacristy, an oven, a coffin, in a triple, fantastic and disagreeable blackness. A possible and an impossible he at the same time.

He used to come to my house. We talked, laughed, thought; he was boisterous and pompous, I exuberant and fiery. It never occurred to me to think about the other. But on leaving, and as he reached that spot on the stairs the abdicating profile, dark, enigmatic, would appear for an instant and leave with him.

XV

The Mechanic from Malaga

We drove out of Málaga with difficulty. The car would stop every other minute, panting. Mechanics from one or another station came by. Each one of them knocked the car here and there with no previous thought; they would pull hard here, say gross words there, sweat in vain. There was no change in the car. We managed with great difficulty to drive to a garage outside of a town whose name I forget, which we were told was very good, on the uphill road to Granada.

The man came out slowly into the morning sun, from the wide, dark depths. He was a tall man, strong, smiling, in control of himself. He looked sure of himself as he approached the car, lifted with precision the lid over the motor, looked inside with exact intelligence, caressed the machine as if it were a living being, knocked with precision the found secret and closed the top of the car with exact rhythm and measure.

"The car is all right. You may drive it wherever you wish."

"Is it really all right? Three mechanics gave up on it earlier as a lost cause."

"All right, really. Lack of proper care. Cars should be treated like animals (he did not say people). Cars need pampering, too."

When we turned around and confidently and peacefully took the high road through the strong and rich June landscape, happy with the grace and work of the good mechanic, I looked back. The mechanic from Málaga was standing by the door, all blue, his hands on his hips, as if accompanying the car with firm complacency.

XVI

The King

The light brown slave appeared suddenly, dressed with feathers and colored robes painted red and white, and jumping among the children. He was singing:

"I was a king in my land; I was a great king and did as I pleased."

Then he would dance, a proud dance, a strong and airy dance. Later he would remove his disguise in front of everyone and leave, carrying it in his hand, for his hut.

He had been a king. But then they trapped him, they hunted him, they stole him and brought him to Puerto Rico as a slave.

He felt like a slave all year round, like a melancholy, poor animal. He was sweet, good, kind. At night he would walk slowly to his hut, would lie down by the door and sing to the stars in unknown words.

But once a year he would suddenly disappear and return, dressed in feathers and colorful robes, and jumping in front of the children, he would sing:

"I was a king . . ."

He would then dance a proud dance, a strong and airy dance.

XVII

The Young Filipino Girl

(Moguer)

She hardly ever left the house: from church to the market, that was all. She would walk very close to the sidewalk, as if stumbling, or as if she were a shadow cut out from the buildings, delicate, almost disembodied, just a frame, coarse and black, allowing only her fine, gray little face with slanted eyes, to show.

She hardly ever talked, though her tiny eyes, black and shining, looked like the seeding ground of delicate words.

Everyone, but especially other girls, made fun of her, imitating her step, her way of talking, of smiling, in a coarse and gross manner which made me think of the coarseness, dullness and heaviness of our Western women.

Some of her neighbors, however, who visited her with some familiarity, used to say: "If you only saw how beautiful she is in her house, and how beautiful her young body is. . . ."

XVIII

The Old Woman

(Moguer)

She was already convalescing and was beginning to move about. No one at home truly loved her. There was only a ritual of love and affection. As a matter of fact they really wished she would finally die, so that they could inherit from her and be free.

The poor woman, unable to surrender to the general distraction, was like a pampered little girl, and would call, in her innocence, everyone's attention with a false voice. When she succeeded in getting anyone to look at her she would then make a gesture, like showing she was able to walk alone, or able to hold to this or that, in the belief that her life was as interesting as that of a child starting to walk.

In return she would receive a few polite words from hypocritical mouths, a few smiles with no sympathy. Thus she kept going, her gaze backwards, with no one casting a glance, through endless rooms, in an effort to reach the dawn, but moving instead, through everyone's effort, towards the cemetery.

XIX

Inner Clearing

(Madrid, Compassion)

Five in the afternoon and the winter sun still shines on
this large, irregular and oblique plot of land which a demolition
team has left looking like a sick town square or like a bold head
with dandruff flakes, or a scalp with ringworms, here in the
midst of the city; a skinny, trodden and dirty grass shows up
through the mounds of earth, and under the light of the sun,
which turns everything sweet, it gives some joy to the soul, a
forced traveler of these spots and witness to the eagerness
with which nature shows up everywhere, to naturalize
everything.

People have left their caves and nests, from high and low,
their hiding places and cellars, and have gathered here
standing, silent and quiet, together and alone in motley filth
and rags to keep company to all the thrown-away things and
the thrown-away uses of the useless and discarded: black
glasses, cloth boots, hats of every description; some of those
present carry on them all they own, summer and winter
superimposed: cape, straw hat, greenish umbrella thrown over
all their fogotten evils; meanwhile the children understand each
other within a society formed under the others, within a
fraternity just below that of true wanderers.

Within this grand and silent solitude which allows one to
listen to the splendid song—sad and contagious—that all
things sing here, the sun begins to die as it melts its tepid gold
in each thing and each being, while at the same time it drowns

itself within the old age of the houses which surrender to it like eternal old women to an eternal young man. The clearing has opened wide to the west the faces of buildings which before were closed in by a street and were, therefore, without sun, or the sun would venture in there obliquely through a side alleyway shining on everything—pharmacies, hairdressing salons, taverns, whore houses—with decrepit, shrill colors as in old, bad paintings filled with dust, cracks and dirt.

XX

The Old Portuguese Man

(New York)

They found him unconscious, in the middle of the immense street, all black, the sclers yellow, and so they took him to the hospital. No one could say anything about him, he had no address or documents. The doctors, disoriented, decided to open him up to find the cause.

"But, are you going to open him up, not knowing why?"

"That is exactly why, because we do not know."

And so they opened him up and as they found nothing they were looking for they closed him up.

The poor old man stayed there in bed, his soul barely held together by the few stitches given him by a hasty and cold doctor.

The next day, in drowsiness, he never stopped complaining and feebly begged:

"Water, water, water."

No one seemed to understand what he wanted.

"For the love of God, a bit of water for this unfortunate man."

The nurse told him the time for water had already passed, it was due at eleven and he had not asked for it then. I said so many things that they finally brought a glass and I gave the water to the old man, who, after he drank the whole glass, smiled at me like saints do.

I asked him about his family and friends or acquaintances, if he wanted me to write a letter to someone in Portugal, or, in America, or wherever.

70

He said:

"No, no, what for? Yes, I have a family, but what for? I am going to die tomorrow, or the day after anyway"—and holding my hand—"When I am in front of God I will remember you, who gave me water."

It did not happen tomorrow or the day after. That same day his white soul left his blackened body by the highway of a spring day, of light, on its way to the God of health and peace.

XXI

Mademoiselle

(Madrid)

She spent the day pairing herself ten times, a day measured by ten pairs; then she would return from those ten pairs made of twenty people to her unique loneliness by retracing a hundred roads n an effort to make either a frozen or a scorching one only. On her way back she walked fast, sliding behind walls and fences, under the solitary sun to avoid being seen in the populated shade, or on foot during a storm so she would not be looked at in the streetcar. She tried to keep herself on the outside, always.

Her street! She lived in a semi-apartment of a semi-house, the rotten backdrop to the hard sun, the blustery wind and the heavy rain. The house served every purpose, from a cave for love to being a photograph of the rising dawn; to get into it from wherever, there was a semi-sidewalk all indented, which would bite the feet; it was filled with odors, colors, shouts, papers, students, liquids, eyes, acid. After that difficult flight following my own nightfall and upon returning to my restful and wide bed I thought of her still entangled in the other nine remaining threads (no knots in any of them) and saw her bearing other people's labyrinths; almost all of the ice and heat were her own, the pain was all hers under the expressionless impassibility of the twenty other impossible characters.

I never knew if she ever had breakfast, or lunch (sometimes we forced her to have merienda with us) or if she had supper during that single and long day which was her life;

nor if she ever slept during that her multiple and brief night. The only thing I know is that she wanted not to be, sweetly stopping from willing in order to stop being; and that her weak, blurred ugliness was always veiled by a wide and kind smile—a useless light that completely covered her old and delicate shrub lit in a constant and spiritual blue flower now faded by sun and running water.

The two of us went together to the white burial. We had to wait a long time, in that valley of cobblestones, under the eyes peeping from all the balconies, because the fly-wing colored horses refused to wear the tuft of burlap, symbol of some kind of purity. There, at the end of the east wing of the cemetery, next to the last hole, from where one could hear the mute fields on the other side, they brought her down into a grave, a very deep grave, deep, deep. I thought: "Now, no messages will reach her; now she will sleep without hunger or thirst, or pain or impertinences." We did not leave. The sky was then turning red over the profiled black silence of the place; the grave digger informed us:

"If you want to wait . . . There are eight more to be thrown over her . . ."

(1917)

XXII

The Odd Old Man

(Madrid)

I would find him, suddenly, anywhere, climbing a lonely staircase, by the window in the landing, within my opened room, by the bridge over the tiny canal, standing next to an ineligible bench. He was tall and albino, wore a wide raincoat, asymmetrically buttoned, long and frayed, the same coat in summer and in winter which allowed only the rigid boots, from somebody else, to show; his eyes were gray-blue, his streaked beard dry, his hands always shaking. I am unable to remember if he ever wore a hat. He used to bring out, from between his flesh and the raincoat, a book on heraldry, under the sun, in the wind, in the snow, wherever it might be, and pointing out shields and crowns no longer golden, told me unintelligible things, in a disjointed Sephardic Castillian.

No one ever saw him come in. But then, when and how did he leave? At night, noon, dawn, afternoon, the old man was there. He looked like a being from some other century (suddenly profiled by some unknown, plastic mirage) unable to communicate with us, though he spoke almost our own words. He was almost true, almost a lie. One was at a loss to figure out what to do with him, accommodate him or dismiss him. Either all or nothing. One felt sorry, he was indifferent, he annoyed. Then, after a brief moment of stray looks and isolated, incongruous phrases, he would leave, where to?, hurriedly.

Sometimes I could see him from my window, erect in the middle of the clearing, his hands thrust into the endless

pockets of his overcoat, the wind cutting out his profile as he turned around—unbecoming, mouldy weathervane—to the four winds. Other times he would stare at the house fixedly. I, then, in the hope of catching the secret of his distant loneliness, would furtively pick up my binoculars and thus bring his face closer to my eyes. His tiny eyes, brought forcibly close, looked at me, fighting back as nails, as insects caught within my glasses, with that private, fixity that smiled incomprehensibly.
(1916)

XXIII

The Cool Violin Player

(Bordeaux)

The old street (stone, water mildew) was alone with the wind; it was a wind with nails, a labyrinth of swords which amused itself by cutting through everything, to make the whole world a martyr. Everyone, on returning home, had closed his door behind him. The bad night was coming on.

Suddenly, with the tiny, first lights from below and the difficult moon in the sky over the river, one could hear the imploring sobbing, at times rending, at others terribly animal, of a well-played violin in the mute street.

She was a young woman, very tall and thin as the bones of a child, well shaped, still delicate, awkwardly dressed in dancing clothes that were once good, faded now and frayed (her collarbone and forearms bare). In that hour of tunes and feelings in upheaval she seemed from another world, another time, than the one she came from. A tiny girl was tugging at the tail of her dress, a thin girl, wide-eyed with a large head, her index finger in her mouth, who laughed not wanting to.

The woman was playing I do not know what, nor for whom, nor for how long; desperate and hungry (every bit of her music said so), forced out of her life, no doubt, to the street (any kind of life, to any street) in a last attachment, a final instinct.

The little girl, believing, no doubt, that all that show was some kind of game (what a tiny carnival!), was looking at the woman, from a little distance, pulling her dress and thus

showing her face to the woman's bare ankles. The little girl, then, looked at me, and laughed; she laughed and laughed not wanting to.
(1916)

XXIV

External Love

(Madrid)

The fresh, hypnotic meadow gathered within itself, as if within its innumerable mauve, purple, blue flowers, a myriad flapping of wings, the bustling of ants' feet, buzzing sounds; one's eyes got lost and returned black and red through the green and blue. Eyes, flowers, grass; eyes, grass, flowers, entwined, fused; grass in the eyes, eyes in the flowers, mourning, sparks. Then, that crazy wind of March seemed to gather and unite in one warm bouquet, as if it were an external heart, the whole spring, the sea, the forests, the skies of the world.

All disheveled and very jagged, an already old woman was crossing the boiling day, dressed in impeccable winter white, all frayed, a heavenly flower in her hand, talking alone, laughing to herself. She stopped, pedagogically, her mouth puckered, her finger straight, and said something sententious to a frightened ant. Here and there, on impulse, almost without looking, as if what she were plucking came from her own distant soul, she would bend over, pluck another blue flower and hide it in her large, faded purse. (My eyes had by now turned by themselves to her place.)

Everything around, on account of the odd beauty imposed by the subjective garden of a lost mind, was throbbing now differently. The wind was raining over the general absence, covered by a zenithal sun, bright tiny leaves of fallen flowers and the last dry leaves forming still a truly melancholic

mixture. The birds, following the timing of the dazzling waves in the water nearby, were crowning with present dreams her delicate quest, as if with old tears, still a little sad, in a confusion of wishing rainbows and infinite gifts filled through love and pain, with spring stones of light.
(1917)

XXV

Old Man Andres

Though the garden with most indifferent sun is filled all around, children, soldiers, widows, this other wild spot of tree trunks with moss and tree trunk shadows which the early afternon inflames in a boundless elegy, is hardly visited by anyone. A ghostly wind isolates it, as if it were a green lake of oblivion.

All its benches continue empty. The near silence is so complete one can hear the non-human confidences that big things, in a low voice, make to the small ones: the sky to the leaves, the air to the birds, the sun to the grass.

Old man Andrés is approaching today with more difficulty, his hand more on his back, more dry, more awkward, more or less; his huge iron buttons larger and his overcoat wider and more immense. (The dead man must have been fully grown and they must have removed the overcoat as he stiffened in the coffin.) He looks as if all the moss in the trees were on his back and the whole shining illness of the sun in his eyes; so much so that in another light he would look like another sad tree, and how much sadder! Everyone knows that to almost all trees red spring returns.

Andrés reaches the antepenultimate bench, not the penultimate, not the last bench; and there all wrapped up within that vegetal hole, within a gold and green cave, he faces the sunset, his sunset where, perhaps, the ray of sun ends, and sits down, laboriously, and carefully at one end.

"The poor man." An odd woman says, after a while. "He

does not dare to sit fully in what is left to him of the bench of life.''
(1905)

XXVI

The Nomad

(Madrid)

On these nights of cold drizzle, a slow-moving old man has the custom of crossing under my balcony playing, nonstop, his bagpipe. He is not a beggar, a drunk, nor is he crazy; he is a peaceful old man from the countryside, who carries within his chest his heart, like a plant in the ground, and up there in his eyes, its flowers.

There are sad men like this one who in order to enchant their loneliness and nostalgia bring with them from their remote villages, a picture, an animal, a blanket. This secretive old man brought with him, no doubt, a sweet bagpipe, filled, like the rocking sea of his coast, with deep music.

On those spent Sunday nights, when there are no more dreams to dream but sleep and when all that was festive is now tired and sleepy, the old man passes under my balcony. He moves slowly like a shepherd leading his tight, ideal herd down a wet slope; he forces the air to speak through his bagpipe, while he moves as if caressed by the musical tune of one of those monotonous morning tunes, wrapped in round fog from the village and the fine flowers and fountains of the open road. The high, closed, black city street is made tender for an instant with the distant softness of the fields of the melodious North; then a child, a woman, a man, open a yellow crack in the wall of their houses and come out into the open which the bagpipe has turned to tears.

Perhaps it is due to the rain falling down again; or the air that feels less frigid, for so does the heart. The old man walks slowly, his eyes lost within his own invisible shadow, holding the bagpipe tightly, playing a ballad of fixed colors and dawns, carrying the fog of hidden valleys, the freshness of an intimate river, the clarity of a familiar sky.

What might the bagpipe tell the slow-moving old man? And he, where is it that he does not want to reach? Would that I were able, as soon as the sweet man came out of his cloud of fog and the bagpipe drowned in silence, just to stand in front of him and bring him his green land, his loving by-paths, his warm porch, and set them all in his hands!
(1901)

XXVII

(Moguer)

They brought Sabinita as a present for the children, an old canary, green and gray-feathered, which belonged to Dona Sabina, an old Castilian. The children went crazy with her for an hour, trying to please her, making gestures; finally they became bored and left her alone. I, then, approached her opened, necessary prison (How are we going to set her free? Where can an old canary go?) and made some funny gestures to her, in my own way:

"Sabinita, pi, pi."

"Sabinita, pi, pi." The canary, a wee bit sad, answered me with the short flight of a lily turned wilted hay on the wires:

"Pi, pi."

All that afternoon, while working, I caressed her with smiles from my poetry. At times I threw words at her or whistles in my pauses, and then with a full reaction:

"Pi, pi."

Sabinita answered me always, her tiny eye joyful, taking to flight suddenly, as a flower that opens instantly looking now less wilted:

"Pi, pi."

Now, already night, Sabinita has hidden her pain under the spongy wing, ready to go to sleep not on the balancing stick, but on a board. Once more my resignation has said: "Pi, pi." Sabinita brings out her green and live eye from her almost white head and answers me, I do not know if from within her dreams or her death:

"Pi . . ."

XXVIII

The Asylum

(Madrid)

They are all gathered there together making brooms with palm leaves and esparto-grass—green yellow in the autumn sun, even yellower over the high, closed courtyard. They wear old dinner jackets with tails, of all makes and sizes, green, brown, gray; hats of all types and ages, straw in winter, summer top hats; unmatchable boots, from the living and the dead. And from within, under, next to all those things, they almost come out.

This is the last courtyard, the one used by the oldest people, and it comes after many other courtyards, where others, not so old, make sandals with hemp soles, mats, baskets, things of greater value. The north wall of their courtyard is closed with an iron fence softened with moss, covering all sight of free land; there are also tiny towers like those in the villages and small trees with sparrows. Through the high iron gates one can see, following one another, funeral carts with the dead, on their way home.

The old people, meanwhile, smooth, clear their throats, pound, cough, cry and swear and then stop and shout and complain about everything human or divine. How many slow-moving old people exposed to the fixed sun which can almost see them with its static light! All this flesh could already have become a current in metamorphosis, for it no longer retains the quality of flesh; it shows a scarred and displeased soul escaping through a thousand openings, weary of its useless body, sweet and sour essence, unable to be contained any longer! These are large cages of dry flesh, of ugly flesh, the ugliest thing in this world and, I suppose, in the next!

The last old people look with disdain and indifference at a passing funeral cart. They seem to be waiting for one afternoon when, at merienda time or during a cigarette break, another more miserable cart than the present one, instead of passing by followed by air and dust, will stop dead by the iron gate. Then, the drunken driver, standing on the driver's seat, will call out to them:

"You! Not you! You!"

(1902)

XXIX

The Aficionado

(Boston)

He used to come every night to the Sommerset Hotel, big and alone, and once the two old people he came to visit had finished dinner, the three would sit near—very near—the quartet, on three easy chairs lined one behind the other, in a salon covered with green velvet.

He, no doubt, came every night—those nights of endless snow!

—from the country, for he smelled of earth and trees, wind and fire. His long face was filled with goodness and optimism, with eyes that were all blue soul and blue face. He was a man resigned to whatever might come, no explanation needed.

He obviously thought he knew about music. He would follow the absurd piece—*Norma, Traviata*—with delighted mimicry, and at times intoxication to the point of standing in a romantic contortion; at the end he would clap vigorously, in the empty salon, and then go and talk for a moment with the musicians, shaking their hands, to find out, by the way, what it was they had played.

Thus, to the end. Then he would thank them, tired and pleased, both musicians and old people, who would pat him on the back paternally; then, opening the door to the furious night, he would leave, erect and slow, like a tree, with an invisible top, filled with breezes and birds.
(1916?)

XXX

The Being of a Profile

(Paris)

This gray being in profile, dressed, held together by pins, walking, fragile, light, stumbling up Cassette Street, simulating a walk within dreams, what weight does he carry in the scale of life?

He moves by the stream of the ugly, dirty and narrow street, sometimes to the right, others to the left, like an eccentric swallow. His clothes bear no name, they do not fill any name as they are not filled by a man. And his being, who would know its name? Green cat, sewer, pink rat. Is he Samain? What is he looking for? Is he looking for himself? Has he lost himself to himself? Has he lost his entity, his existence, his past, his future, his present?

I follow him through Vaugirard Street, the iron fences of the Luxembourg, again up Cassette Street. The same mistake, the same single profile, at Rennes Street, at Cassette again. How can he have only one side? Who knows? Maybe Jules Renard, but he is also dead.

The afternoon is colorless other than blackened, filthy, silent streets. That wall with illustrious soot of the imperial house becomes exalted with the light of its tall and round balconies. The convent of the condemned, its ghostly elm trees quiet, is gathering its evil green. The yellowish rat, the blue cat, the stinking drain of the obscene sewer, parallel spouts, are the natural accompaniments of the humid August sunset. And that cloud, and those trailing stars, and how sad Verlain must be at the Luxembourg?

I refuse to follow the man of only one profile. I am tired. Saint Sulpice Square. A widow's bench. I find distraction for a moment thinking of Boileau and Mallarmé.

When my eyes start to see again they see that the little being is looking at me with the eye from the other wide, which I never saw before.

(1936)

XXXI

The Integral Horticulturist

(Havana)

It is my wish that before the mango season is over you try these few, gathered with the morning freshness.

This fruit is known in classical terms as *passiflora quadrangularis,* which in this country is translated as pomegranate and in Moguer resembles a small melon.

He reminded me of his father, or rather, I thought it was his father I saw when as a child in Moguer he came to our house often, always in a hurry, dressed as a mason, his work on his shoulders, his green and violet eyes, almost blind from seeing inwardly and distantly, sunk in his head.

He would tell us of his life, with his violet and green eyes sunk all the way into his deepest, ultimate being—his ideal abyss—and while his hands, sinewy, heavy and restless were in the water, like a pendulum of power, or upon a leaf or a stone. He seemed to caress everything with his intense, wandering eyes and in turn, everything—trees, seeded fields, flowers, the well—seemed to respond joyfully, as if bending to this side or that under the imaginative timing of their gardener, their horticulturist, their lover. He decribed every detail to me with exquisite delight and named the produce with their Latin names and then added their current, Cuban name. He would then say: "This is what in Moguer is called . . ." In the background one could see the wooden, small house, almost made of nature, with the bed almost coming out of the window, and books. Then: "Here, take this rose for your wife, and this tiny plant of sweet basil, and this mango, and . . ."

While still very young in Moguer he became angry with his father. One morning, saying nothing to his father, and carrying nothing, except what he was wearing, he took the road to San Juan del Puerto and "taca, taca, taca," he left for Sevilla. There he hid in the hold of a ship from the Ybarra Company and left for England. The captain discovered him on the high seas, excused him and requisitioned him, "taca, taca, taca," to work on board the ship. Then another ship and he went to Buenos Aires. "Taca, taca," to California. Finally, Cuba, "taca." He crossed these seas many times: a biscuit in his knapsack, a casual fountain and "taca, taca, taca." Where night caught him there he laid horizontal and went to sleep. With the first sun, "taca, taca, taca," and "taca, taca, taca" with the beautiful moon, too.

The first sun and the beautiful Cuban moon. "She" then, appeared: his naturalist, poetess wife, behind the well. She appeared warm, the image of a gazelle, quiet, her two pigtails parallel over the flat chest, wearing a yellow and pink scarf over her white tunic. She reminded me of the crying *Verónica* in the procession of Moguer's Holy Week. She did not come close to us. She raised her arm and pointing to the light, raised her voice like a tiny dove: "He is an adventurer, and has travelled everywhere, yes, sir, but . . ." her voice then became a cross made of swords, "he has managed to keep his innocence."
(1937–39)

XXXII

*The People from Jijona at Christmas**

*Note: Jijona: a town on the eastern coast of
Spain that produces special Christmas
sweets and candies.

    Within the white confines of the shop, where a feeble
lilac-yellow gas light fuses edges and corners into a single
plane, the young man from Jijona, seated, quiet and lean,
projects his hard black profile as if he were in a different space.

    One could believe it was his own nostalgia that was placed
behind the cloth counter, that was the demented salesman;
that it was his own being, as dreamed in solitude by himself,
sad, far away, in joyful Jijona, next to his light and soft wife in
those antecedent autumn nights that ushered in December.
The melancholic profile does not seem to be interested in
selling his nougat candy, nor his sweet almonds; it just lies
there with everything else, in case those that pass by feel like
commiserating—him being here in Madrid, cold and lonely,
fulfilling a ritual from the east coast.

    (Through the main square people come and go: dull
maids, burlapy old people, fathers with their children, slow-
moving soldiers alone with their sabers. A large and cold moon,
appearing through recently raining clouds, gathers into itsglobe
the whole world by attracting the wider eyes, those of
astrologers, with its well-defined, beautiful immensity. As she
comes and goes in and out of the stormy clouds, everything
becomes confused, in painful revolution, against her

background. One could say that high things are not in their place and not attending to their task; that everything has become the useless and ungrateful landscape of sadness.)

In a low water trough, in front of the shop from Alicante, the still and shining waters wave constantly; people say it is good for drinking (yes, yes, used to say that shameless priest from Jaen) for those who suffer from neurasthenia. Silently the yellow clock, red also and tarnished under the frozen, radiant moon, turns this corral of Madrid into a sentimental no-time place with its any-time hour. Meanwhile the young man from Jijona, black, still as a nail, his soul on the alert, facing the poor water, remains seated under moon and clock, not seeing, listening or speaking, right in the center of his white, wide shop.

Is that the sound of an absorbed bagpipe, of an enchanted guitar? There is within his deep silence a certain melodious plenitude that moves. One could think, at the sound of that secret tone, that what he is really selling is his own life, which lies in front of him dead in little pieces, within boxes of light wood. Yes, this is it: it all looks like a child's funeral wake.

The young man from Jijona continues, hour after hour (midnight?) of the red clock, seated, black (Oh, dead Manet and live Picasso over there in France!) in the deep, white shop. (1916–20)

XXXIII

Double Man

I met him on a pleasant afternoon, playing the piano,
standing near him in the gray and sweet penumbra of a spring
sunset, at his home. He seemed to me, then, sweet, good,
simple, his heart throbbing with the music of his piano, among
his children, his wife and his flowers.

On the following day, however, in his office, from far
away, as I entered through the distant door of the large bank, I
thought I had confused him with another, somebody else. He
looked thinner, darker, bent over legal papers and linoleum, his
tiny pepper eyes in no way resembling the blue eyes of the
previous day; the tiny eyes looked at me, as I approached, with
displeasure.

As I reached a certain spot in the room, as it sometimes
happens with trees as we approach them, or as if there had
been a theatrical sleight of hand, the man I was looking at
today, the office-man, became transformed again into
yesterday's man, the piano-man, and a wide and soft smile
replaced the narrow, hard and unpleasant looks in him.

He must have noticed my confusion, and I told him what
it was:

"I did not recognize you for a moment. I thought you were
someone else."

He laughed with a hard laughter, as if he knew the secret
of my doubt, a laughter I could not place as either good or evil,
for I did not know to which one of "the two of them" it
belonged, to the sweet piano-man laughing at my suspicion, or
to the annoying bank-man, laughing at my unhappiness.

. . . His wife read this written page, and suddenly she shivered all over and let out a sharp shriek.

She was not the only one with the dark suspicion. The poet had seen it too. In her house there lived two men.
(1920)

XXXIV

The Elements

As the first drops of rain started to fall by the power of the twisted, immense, round and lightning cyclone—thunder next to light
—he entered the house hurriedly, closing the door behind:

"What a foul afternoon it has turned out to be! Raise the window blinds! What a strong wind! We are in for a terrible storm!"

Inveterate fear of the first man facing natural phenomena with no names!

Horror of water, earth, wind, fire, still lacking millenial names!

Man, however, has proceeded to domesticate the things around him, almost at will; despite an occasional bite, they have surrendered to him like domesticated animals.

(1924)

XXXV

Girls at Play

(Compassion)

The poor, young girls of Madrid, are uglier, more unhealthy-looking than those in Andalucia; they have had more illnesses, their diet is not as healthy; their games are sadder and their voices, like tiny water sprinklers from even more depleted fountains, sound more full of earth.

The songs they sing are the same. A bit longer, more learned, more emphatic with precocious feeling, less romantic passion, and less sad joy. It is apparent to me now that when these young girls become women, they will exchange the present games for the docile pairing at the bullring or the dancing hall.

These girls will become the women—pale, full of shadows and humidity—of a printer, a bookbinder, of . . . . Oh, no, alas! Why not the woman of a cooper, a stable boy, a wine maker, a harvester, a fisherman, a farmer, the woman of all those labors that, though they are poor, have a window to the water, the fields, the light. But no, this is not possible, alas! It is not possible for her song, which today is the happy seed of her small heart, to be transformed into a spring afternoon with grape-vines, blue plant-pots and the sails of ships, white, pink, pure breeze, all clean and clear!

They sing:

"Ramón of my soul . . ."

There is more light now in the street, enchanting a little the feeling of the night that is now coming. Someone calls the girls from the tavern, the fishery, the printing shop, the caretaker's window; everything feels humid, confused, and gives out a bad odor.

They keep singing as they go:

"Ramón of my soul . . ."

Poor Ramón of Madrid, bookbinder, printer. . . . He is at play today with girls and poor little women who already belong to Ramón.

(1915)

Part III

Long Stories

I

Long Stories

Long stories! That long! One page long! When will the day come when people will learn to lengthen a spark all the way to the sun from a sun gathered within a spark given to them by a man; the day we all realize nothing has size and that, therefore, what is sufficient is enough; the day we understand that things do not gain their worth from their size—this would put an end to the ridiculous attitudes seen by Micromega* and that I see daily—(the day) when a whole book may be reduced to the size of an ant's hand, for an idea may enlarge it and turn it into the universe!

*Fictitious character which combines the perspective of the smallest and of the end.

II

Austere Pain

Brother, we are unable to go; we have nothing we can send you, not even for the burial, neither flowers, nor candles. But you know this pain shrinks us, constrains us, pales us, to the point of making us wear around the house old clothes dyed black, like shadows.

We eat in silence, work in silence, in silence we walk to the window to see the cloudy sea; we sit awhile by the door, we go to sleep and in silence we do not sleep.

Since none of us has anything left over, we feel no obstacle comes between us who live on this earth as in a broken-down and sad, poor barn.

And the three of us, you there, the two of us here, surrounded by naked walls and poor things share the great consolation of believing we are all together with her, in death.

III

A Voice

She was just a voice. A voice that one day asked me on the phone: "I wish to see you, know you. Would you like me to come over?"

I answered: "O.K., but when you return."

She left, returned and died without my knowing it. For me she became only a voice. But this voice which belonged to her, is *she*, who no longer is.

IV

The Son

I would hide, and you would keep looking for me, looking for me.

Tired at last, since you could not find me, you would get a little angry and would say: "Son, come out at once. This is no longer a game!"

Then you would leave. And I would peek out a little bit from my hiding place, laughing.

Now you have hidden, and how well! And I cannot find you.

I look and look for you, and feeling the coming of night, very sad, I ask you: "Mother, come out at once. This is no longer a game!"

I come and go alone. And you, do you peek out, smiling, from your hiding place?

V

Yellow Leaves

> "Look through the silver poplars . . ."

Yesterday's children, who with the joy of the coming green climbed those silver poplars of Moguer towards the sky, today, under these same poplars and as they anticipate the coming of the earth to cover them, they fall down, all yellow, through the branches. They are beginning to feel as if they were held together only by the spirit.

One morning we find them on their backs lying down upon a dead heap of gold.

VI

Without Name

    I like to think of you with no name or surname; just a woman, as a cloud is a cloud.

    (I like to think of you) running within the blue air, your blonde hair waving upon your violet and white flesh, by the water, under the green birds.

    (I like to think of you) only as a woman, with no signs of now, as a rose is a rose.

VII

Frighteningly Happy

I was a soul in pain, lost as a madman, and so I let out a howl to the open summer fields.

My voice echoed against a solitary red rock. It sounded like an escaped heart within the fearful labyrinths of an echo never heard before.

The rock became alive with my howl. It became a large frenetic face looking at me joyfully, listening to me joyfully, answering me joyfully. Frighteningly happy, she responded:

"Son of the great mother! Voice, my daughter; daughter of my own voice!"

VIII

Confused Words

  The sick young girl did not allow him to think or to sleep; to think towards sleep, to sleep thinking and dreaming.

  She opened, cut up, dissected his thoughts and sleep with her constant hiccup, the whistling of her nose, her choking, the scarce and modest necessities she needed to perform for her to be able to sleep and dream.

  He spoke to her in the most affectionate manner:

  "My child, see if you can fall dead asleep finally and completely."

  Unfortunate choice of words. Using the misunderstood sentence as her fatal destiny she heard only: "Fall dead finally and completely!"

  She died. He did not perceive in the blue and black shadows the power of the misguided sentence which the young girl had lodged in her weak head like a bullet. She did fall dead asleep forever.

  (That night destiny filled the world.)

IX

The Blind Father

Since he was unable to see they placed him in a tiny room under the staircase. "Saint Job!" they called him, laughing.

His heart was sick and he thought sadly of his machine that had become out of order, bearing with smiles that dark, invisible and great weight on his life. Had he been able to open his eyes and see that weight he would have stepped on it and crushed it, out of anguish, in an instant.

The rest of the house was full of useless, sunny rooms, with mirrors and birds and balconies where his daughters would spend their time spying on army officers and pianolas.

X

Woman in Love

I never managed to see the eyes of the druid. I saw everything else, but not the eyes; she was white, tender, gray, submissive, delicate. Suddenly, she turned around and left, her arms over her hair, her eyes clouded.

How much whirling beauty! Yet, the more I think about her and her beauty, the only thing I remember well are her eyes.

XI

The Child in the Sea

On some autumn afternoons, women sit sewing by the doors of their houses, under the pleasant and warm sun of the grape harvest. They can see the shore from their chairs and rising above the Angustias the shining line of the sea. One poor mother would leave her sewing from time to time. Her eyes would become lost on the horizon, herself transformed in a new life and new beauty. Suddenly she would shout:

"Look how beautiful my son looks, all gold and laughing!"

XII

The Timid Gesture

He was always ready to do anything. How helpful, how good, how ready he was. His vocation was to serve everyone, work for everyone. Obviously, everyone asked him to do more. If he ever made a mistake we threw it in his face, we counted it against him, sometimes even if he did not make a mistake.

When he did something he thought might make us angry or annoy us he took himself to a corner, all shrivelled up, his eyes sunk to the point of not being round any more. Then, as if speaking from the shadows he said: "Please, excuse me for not having done this, and this and this!"

When he died his face retained his apologetic gesture as if in miniature. His eyes were half opened, half closed and they seemed to speak up to all of us, as a shadow chasing the light:

"Please, forgive me for being dead!"

XIII

The River

    This is the true river, dreamt love. You are in nothingness, I in life. Time alone is all that runs between the two of us.

    The two shores are the same, but the one can hardly be seen from the other, now that the river runs so wide.

    The river will narrow, though. I will see you, dreamt love, and I will cross the river and will remain with you forever. (1913)

XIV

The Funeral

Your cortege moves on slowly, long, indifferent, like a
thick ant swarm of whispers, or like a huge worm all cut up
(ugly chunks) by a flight of bells with light, live crystal and a
creek with new bushes. It moves under the flight of a shining
airplane turning towards the pink south, now showing yellow,
though it is still blue. You are all black within your last lining,
wrapped in fresh green and water all transparent by the pure
sun. You are totally silent within the sound of bells that almost
speak and a little buried before you reach the earth under the
shadowy wings of the tall, live man.

I turn a moment towards you, you, whoever you might be
(a friend for an instant, a face seen somewhere, a complete
stranger?). I must go this afternoon for a while to do my
cloistered obligation surrounded by spring. Good-bye to you,
then, silent one, horizontal one, dark one.

(1914)

XV

Atrophied Memory

I left it every day for the next. It was the kind of memory I did not want to stop remembering well but which I never had the time to remember completely. Since I did not wish to remember it badly I never remembered it.

I felt at ease for I knew the memory was safe in me remembering itself; as if it were a solid object that took care, without my will, of not using the eraser of forgetfulness. As when we make a knot in a handkerchief, so my memory had made a knot day after day on itself.

One day when I felt I had the time I lay down on my unoccupied sofa, as I usually do in such cases, to remember my memory. It was not possible for me to remember it any more. It was in me and yet it was hard, heavy, dry like stale bread, a bone, a callus in my thought, letting out a fossil pain, like a useless obstacle of forgetfulness.

(1916)

XVI

The Possessed

He is in his room getting dressed for a funeral and running late.

While putting on his pants, shoes, tie and vest, he feels tempted and drawn by general thoughts with greater and more demanding urgency than the first urgency. But he suddenly discovers on a door a nail. It is half out, straight, shining, exact, perfect. He feels drawn to hammer that nail, though the nail needs no hammering. He holds in his hand a wooden hanger for his coat, a wooden hammer which appears so tempting to nail down a tempting nail. He forgets the funeral, puts aside his general thoughts, picks up the wooden hanger and starts to hammer down, with slow care, the nail.

(1922)

XVII

Vigilance

    In the middle of the unknown city, after an afternoon of boredom and loneliness, I suddenly find myself in a known place, though I had not seen it before.

    The early moonlight reflected on the artificial light of the houses as if I had been born in one of them. The people rushing to take the buses looked like the people from the village where I was born.

    I felt warmth and peace, as if a moving, immense womb belonging to an infinite, itinerant mother had just come to me without my knowing and had placed me in its white and beautiful nest.

(1922, February 2nd)

XVIII

Night

That dog, now barking, has come out of nothingness; he will return to nothingness.

That girl, now singing, has come out of nothingness and she will return to nothingness.

That water, now running, has come out of nothingness and will return to nothingness.

That pearly moon has come out of nothingness and will return to nothingness.

You, too, woman who loves me, have come out of nothingness and will return to nothingness.

I, too, woman who loves me, who am writing these words, have come out of nothingness and will return to nothingness. (1922, December)

XIX

The Poet

Une belle vie, c'est une pensée de
la jeunesse realisée dans l'âge mûr.*
Alfred de Vigny

One day, fed up at last of so much doubt and martyrdom,
he told himself: "I will no longer take my thoughts to the idle
sofa and caress them infinitely; no more dreams and no more
contemplatng what has been done, what is being done and
what will be done!"

"I will pretend I died and that another I, freed from myself,
is born and able to isolate my work in new drafts. I have, after
all, thought, contemplated, dreamt enough. True aristocracy
consists in not contemplating, not dreaming, not thinking the
same thing twice!"

All became filled with inner, large joy of eternal spring.
Crazy with this definitive idea, singing through the windows to
the sun of the blue morning he decided to put it into practice at
once. . . . Then he took it to the idle sofa to caress it infinitely.
(1922–24)

* A good life is a thought of youth that is only realized in one's mature years.

XX

Daily Beauty

The ticket collector gave the rider of the streetcar a tiny violet stub mixed with the copper change. The violet stub appearing between a penny and a nickel looked like a cute, fresh, secret, pressed flower.

"Violet and copper," he said, shouting within his soul now raised by the naked spring afternoon whose waves the happy streetcar was breaking like a dolphin breaks the choppy sea of his love: "You certainly are everywhere, Beauty, the one goddess who is forever mine!"

(1922–24)

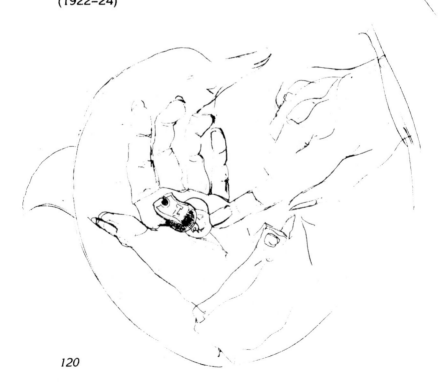

XXI

The Smooth, Gray Eraser

    As we reached the definitive street corner he told me suddenly and all at once (as if the seconds had shrunk, and he was not able to figure out how, or like the sudden ring of an alarm clock, or the lightening of a mirror?):

    "I have no paper in my memory. Thus I do not know from where my inner cold comes, nor where it is I am dreaming, nor what I should do on land or sea. I do not even know why you and I are here, looking so similar, under this sun or that moon."

    Then I suddenly realized why it was that my acquaintance had that smooth, gray eraser instead of a face.

(1922–24)

XXII

The Man with Gout

1.

Annoyance—hyperaethesia—boredom, disgust at art, science, lies, truth, the street, friends, home, life, nakedness, death.

What was he up to, that convex sunset over the doomed planet, all red and black, objectively charming?

He entered a shining bakery and bought himself rich, treasured sweets, making sure to choose those that would harm him the most.

2.

The Little Papers

The need to look always behind and under in case some paper has fallen down. To look, morning and night, under the furniture. To feel the compulsion to make notes everywhere, in the margins of newspapers and therefore the need to keep them. To look, when sweeping in the garbage, in case some little papers are there. Horrible suffering.

3.

The excitement caused in me by such compulsion forces me to live, work, etc., with a different rhythm from that of my heart. I swear I suffer from an immense tachycardia; I take my pulse: 72, 74, 76, at the most. But there is within me another rhythm, another "pulse," I know not where, that hurries me on.

4.

The Repetition

The need to repeat everything two or three times; to look inside a room, clothes, etc., for signs of fire in the belief that I did not do it properly.

The need to repeat in thought all the acts of the day, to get out of bed, wash, etc.

Horrible suffering.

5.

Fixed Ideas

Everything became in him a fixed idea: reading from the newspapers, the list of accidents. He made a mental composition seeing the place in everything. He needed to make himself present everywhere and become a spectator or a hero in every happening.

His was the martyrdom of transporting from each night to the following day the load of fixed ideas and feelings.

Then, they would disolve by themselves. They would die like fireworks, blackened after their explosion that became lost in the night.

6.

The Young Man with Gout

A poet with gout (where and when) will he pick up this book to calm down, as I, alas, have picked up other books, so many!

Yes, be at peace and work. Pierce with your spiritual light all those flying flies; muffle with celestial tunes the crickets in your ears; plant a strong tree against your seasickness.

Do not hurry up your work for anything; be in no hurry even when death is around the corner. Take a bit, each day, from the very best, this will bring you a drop of the good, of synthesis and selectivity.

Think, poet with gout, that delayed pleasure feels better in the present, as much as does the frequent pleasure in the past and enjoy this spring with intensity, in case it were the last, and not with sorrow, in case it were not.

XXIII

The Secret Face

That face, the one with thirteen thousand odd and evident faces, has stopped today staring at me with only one, limpid, strange face. What a face! Has it climbed out of the undredged deep, like a magic sea-monster of the impossible, or has it been no more than the unbelievable light mixed with a demented shadow that have come together as her surface?

It was a face whose beauty I understood at once as not ever being comprehensible. I knew how to think about those other thirteen thousand virginal faces, all of them familiar, but not about this extreme, alert face, which stared, fixed and annoyed, at my own, like a shining being appearing through a mistake of the gods or the elements upon a foreign beach.

The saddest thing is not to think of the mystery of this unique, incomprehensible face, but rather to think of the infinite, negative, dead faces that that face dropped somewhere, all broken up into unconscious essences, useless to the good or evil of a naked sunset, sharing the secret (a one-day crystal) that has already melted away into nothing and which I will never be able to fathom or decipher.
(1922–24)

XXIV

The Street

    That white bitch that only yesterday was clean and playful under the happy spout of water, beneath the green hanging branches! The spring sun was shining on her beautiful, live features. We, then, looked at her, she looked at us.

    Tonight I found her lying under a street light. I called her. She did not move. I touched her, she did not move. (The gaslight [lonely and sad whistle] shines on her sweet, dead features.) I looked at her, she did not look at me.
(1922–24)

XXV

Words

She resurrected from the deep vein of mined centuries, strangely beautiful and different, magic exemplar of an extinguished species: original, middle and last; black, golden, white, gray; sharp and round; complete like poetry; she wore the triple, undefinable prestige of a different woman, a millenial heroine, an ex-dead.

In the beginning she did not want anything to do with us. Like a gazelle, a dragon-fly, a dove, she would retreat herself into a corner using her hands for defense, or she would try to turn around, strangely beautiful and different towards her lower ground. She had an inconceivable charm in her fright, in her manners, in any of her many forms.

Little by little she began to move toward us. She approached our table, our fire; she went to sleep in her bed, almost totally naked. She started to play with the youngest children, to let out almost clear shouts, to laugh and cry like them, strangely beautiful and different. One day, at last, she spoke, just like we do.
(1922–24)

XVI

The Quiet One

As soon as he was able to conquer, after so long, the terrible, draining inquietude of noise, then he had to take on that of his temperature. Then, in succession, that of the light, the hour, the telephone, the visitors, the close contact. . . . He conquered them all.

He was about to become happy in his own way (and that of Kant) when he felt again the invincible disquietude of feeling guilty because of the conquered quietude.
(1923–24)

XXVII

Basilio

He was saying, under the white and green porcelain lamp
in his dining room, with all the signs of a mistaken man:
"Where are now, my friend, all those Basilios; the Basilios of
every afternoon; the Basilios I shared my youth with, my
adolescence and, yes! the Basilios of my childhood!"

As he was thus speaking I saw a five-year-old child I
confusedly remembered from when I was six years of age
climbing over his curved chair from Vienna, I know not from
where it came, and peer at his face laughing.
(1923–24)

XXVIII

The Grape Harvester

The grape harvester was climbing, tired under the round weight, squeezed between the earth and an immense, unique, waving cluster of grapes. I shouted at him from my seat as a guest to watch the early morning grape harvest:

"What a bunch, neighbor, what a bunch!"

Then I approached him to touch a grape of a different color, a red grape, in a gesture of exaggeration as if to compensate. As if the shivering inconvenience of the early hour (outlined on land with patent leather and black dyes against a sharp metallic green background) were a possible offense on my part to that brute human, within this forgotten village and with a presumed, unknown woman.

Far away? Near? As if within an auditive mirage, we could hear the first morning tramway, moving on endlessly, with a beautiful noise of empty gas cans.

(1926)

XXIX

The New One

She became confused looking at her. She was almost identical to herself. But I knew well she was not the same one.

She never fought against her substitute. Thus her colorless eyes, her thin waist, her smooth hair, her most unmistakable graces began to melt away, forgotten in those of the soft, smiling and invading being, to the point of her total annihilation. It seemed like a total transfusion of a soul.

As I started walking away after my sad testimonial, I felt under my left shoe (I could not avoid it even though I raised my foot instantly) a crunch, as when one steps on a useless thing, a shell.

(1926)

XXX

Time

 We were just talking an instant ago: "In twenty years, when I will be forty-five . . ." Suddenly, that feeling of not being well, the diminished clarity of thought, a light and shadow flying away from each other, the hand over the eyes. Not knowing why, we find ourselves saying:

 "Twenty years ago, when I was twenty-five . . ."

 What has happened in between, in that dubious, unshrinkable, incomprehensible instant?

 Nothing, just that, time.

(1927)

XXXI

The Straight One

He had the heroic, beautiful mania of keeping everything straight, right, square. He spent the day straightening out, in an exact correspondence of lines, pictures, furniture, carpets, doors, screens. His life was an unbearable suffering and a terrible waste. He used to follow after family members and servants, patiently and impatiently, setting in order what they had left in disorder. He knew well the story about the man who had his one good tooth removed from the right side of his mouth because a bad tooth had to be removed from the left side.

When he was about to die he begged, in a weak voice, that they should place his bed in an exact line with the chest, the closet, the paintings, the medicine boxes.

When he died and was buried, the gravedigger left his box in the tomb crooked forever.

(1930)

XXXII

Deceived Girl

Her mother had promised her an orange if she did what her mother wanted. The little girl did it with a smiling effort. Then the mother, her teeth and eyes in a burst of indecent laughter, ate the orange and threw the skin to the little girl.

The little girl picked up the skin and stared through the window (at God?).

A word from a different world lodged in her throat. Her eyes, as if a dose of all the pain of her life had climbed early into them, or as if they had seen, lived, all of her life in one split second, stared—fixed, thick, discarded lead—like those of an old woman.

(1931)

XXXIII

The Gesture

The ugly one, the old one, had stolen from the young one, the beautiful one, her best gesture. She had done it with such skill that with that stolen gesture she had become more the other one than she was herself.

Little by little she became more, more, more beautiful with that gesture of the young one. The beautiful one became more, more, more ugly, more gray, more dry, deprived of her own gesture.

The beautiful one, the ex-beautiful one, remained as if she had lost her treasure. She became ill, she made her gesture become flat, then she wrinkled it, then she did the same with its memory. She died.

The gesture, the stolen one, the treasure, remained for the duration of its life, as one of those inherited jewels from a woman of prestige in the hands of a nobody. It was not able to shine any more or show its colors except in the hands of her unique mistress.
(1933)

XXXIV

Green Secret

The green color that hides in your eyes, the one that comes out at times when your face is flushed with emotion or tears, it is the green color of your eternity.

I know that color green will be my joy and my guilt. You were a miser with it; you gave it to me only in the best of love or in the most intense pain.

Someone told me: "She lets out such beautiful color green only when she blushes!" Beautiful color green! Green color that came out, or indeed came out all it could, or perhaps, all it wished.

(1941)

XXXV

Long Stories about Words

1.

Words and Kisses

The new month was born with a dull, fresh, close, foggy face that let out here and there blue glances and golden smiles.

(He said) I would like to press all of my face against all that immense, opaque and luminous face and kiss in it the whole universe.

And as the man said this, a red sun, like a kiss, opened up everything in smiles among the enchantment of the fascinated fog.

2.

Creation

The blind man was pronouncing and repeating these words: rose, water, wind, in an ecstatic and smiling joy. To him they were almost the things themselves, the elements of a universe that he and she were creating.

As is the starry sky, for those who see, so it was for him the world of words.

3.

Her Handwriting

She had never written to me. Oh, the enchantment of the unexpected handwriting!

This was her first letter; the first letter of a beloved woman of whom we know everything, everything except her handwriting. This handwriting is the daughter of that arm that rested, like a long, soft and warm flower upon our shoulder; it is the daughter of that hand we covered with our kisses; it is a thin handwriting, as delicate as the blink of her golden eyelashes; it adds now one more miraculous grace to all her other graces.

Handwriting kept in reserve! It is a silence that suddenly becomes a sigh, or smiles like a wheat field, or sobs or cries like a stream, or kisses like a mouth.

Hidden handwriting! My kisses were missing in you, for they never before could kiss you in your absence.

4.

The Offended Word

He had a habit of reading over his writing after he had dictated it to the typist; this was his first correction. That day he did not correct the poem for lack of time or desire. In that poem there hid a word that was waiting to be corrected with love. And the second draft passed with the confused word in it to the waiting pile.

Months later, one restless morning, he reached for the poem thinking of the exact inexactitude. The first thing he saw on looking at it was the mistake, the word that did not belong there. He tried to remember the word that belonged there, but he could not; he tried to the right, he could not; to the left, he could not; upside, downside, on its edge, against a different light, translating the word into French, English, Portuguese, Catalan, Galician; he tried sitting on the patio where he first felt the poem, then on the other place where he dictated it. . . . Never again was he able to find that honest word, the obedient word of fidelity.

Yes, that miserable and faithful word had truly become offended. In its offense it had hidden inside its fidelity and truth forever; it had left the poem forever and it had left the poet too; it left them without her, both broken down, filled with holes, forever disunited.

5.

Tone and Word

When that first man was no longer able to say what he felt he started to sing; first like an idiot, in the end a crazy man, that first, senseless man. Thus he invented music.

He sang till he was unable to continue. Then, already calmed down, also empty of musical notes at last, he felt he had a few words left over. They went more or less like these: "To become shipwrecked on this sea feels sweet." Or these words: "May I live within a shell and be the king of infinite space, were it not for my bad dreams." Or these: "The poet is changed by eternity just as much as he changes himself."

Words, after all, are greater than music. Words are the most, the end, and not as some have believed up to now, "in the beginning."

6.

A Poem, at Times, Need Not Be Written Down

It was good, even magnificent. Others are written down but this poem was not.

There was no reason at all for not writing it down, and yet, this one was not.

From that day on, on days mostly of feeling low, that poem hurts, tastes bitter, feels like martyrdom and yet it is not written down.

If one were to write it down it would put an end to everything, and yet it is not done.

And yet, the poem wants to come out, it wants to live, be enjoyed, become eternal; but one is good, one does not write it down.

Part IV

Natural Crimes

I

*A Justification**

I said (and they were all listening) that it had been a secret desire of my whole life to find a person, someone equally similar, a resemblance, a different person, an enemy, man or woman, who would tell me the absolute truth of his or her existence, his or her life; no doubt would be allowed to diminish from that truth the possibilities of what remained uncovered or hypocritical; a human who would allow me to know his, her life as I know mine. For (I continued) I would not like to leave this general world, or my particular life, not knowing a human reality in its completeness, besides my own. But I would not care for a person whose love or interest could deceive or mislead him or her.

There were gestures, smiles, exaggerated moves, changes and evasiveness. And I took it that the end of that question arrived with my final period. But on the following day, the question of the previous evening's conversation, already forgotten, for the time being, I received a feminine phone call. The woman said:

"You said yesterday, and I heard it, that it had been a secret of your whole life to find a person that would narrate to you the absolute truth of her life; someone whose life you would come to know as you know yours.

"I have been on the verge of killing myself several times, bored with the conventional and because I found no justification whatsoever for my existence. I have come to believe, to convince myself that I am of no use to anyone or for anything. Yesterday, as I listened to you, a light suddenly and

143

completely illumined me; for now I think, feel and believe that I
have a justification for my life, or even better, *the* justification:
to narrate, to someone who wishes to know, the absolute life of
another, my own. I wish to give, thus, usefulness, or perhaps
beauty, or perhaps Interest with my life to someone who has
desired to taste, to know, to know me."

The woman came to visit. She was a woman of about
forty years, her ivory façade in ruins and yet still erect like a
wavering candle. After she smiled at me and was seated,
without any prologue, with complete assurance in her eyes and
voice, without any shadow of evasion, of doubt, of
impertinence, vanity or humility, she told me simply and
clearly her life. It took no more than an hour, an hour filled like
a treasure, an hour treasured by her, a treasurer; an hour of
beautiful truth and made up of only what was necessary. One
hour, a full treasure and no thought about the work done. It was
the exact content of a determined container. A natural
masterpiece without metaphorical comparison or infantile
fantasy.

I told her, without commentary too: "Write it down."

"I do not know how to write," she answered definitively,
"nor do I care to learn how, or to write it." . . . If I were able to
put down, repeat what she told me, in her own words, or my
own that would repeat her own accent, her exact attitude, the
whole look in her eyes, I would write a true book, the most
beautiful and naturally strange; even more, I would write a
round world not able to dream or conceive by myself. But I
cannot even try. I know it would be impossible for me to write it
down. I know that this rare jewel of a human life, at once
conscious and instructive, sensitive and thoughtful, that truth
told without support, will forever remain inlaid within my own
substance, within my own hidden mine, like irreplaceable gold,
for it would turn into a fossil of gold in my attempt to transform
it into writing. And, perhaps, it would turn out, besides, against
my own wish, that I would be committing a natural, individual
and collective crime.

Anyway, I know for sure I have justified a secret, beautiful and dignified life. And that I have done so through a few sincere words I said. And I know above all that I know and own a marvelous oral story that no one else besides me will ever know. For she told me:

"My life is now justified, and needs no more. Even though someone else, a most improbable thing, would like to know it, what would I gain with two people knowing it? This would remove quality to my justification. If you now have my life, because you deserved it, I also feel that I deserve that you have it. I know I would not be able to justify it in the same manner, again. Besides I know now I am complete. I needed, not a friend, nor a lover, nor a husband, but someone who would complete me.

"Now," she concluded before leaving forever, "now we are two mirrors, glass against glass. Both copy each other like a river and the sky, both unable to know now whose reflection was the first to appear. You have me reflected in your mirror and I have you in mine. This is what I wanted: mutual reflection. This unity of closed comprehension, these two mirrors stuck to each other make everything dark on the outside, but on the inside there is immense luminosity, my immensity."

* From *Natural Crimes*, this is a sketch of a novel I would have liked to write.

II

Memory's Accidents

1.

This Is No Longer Possible

I will not go; no, I will not see it.

In order to see it as I dream of it I would have to become the child who would have also been the man I am now. This is no longer possible!

If I now went on my feet to see it, the dream I have as a man would die too; the dream of how that could have been seen by me as a child who has also been the man I am now. This is no longer possible!

It is not possible! That will remain what it was and I will be unable to see that I am not seeing it; I will not be able to go back nor see it. It will never be what it could have been if I, a child, had been also the man I am now. This is no longer possible!

2.

The Fifth Layer

It is all right! The first layer has already become a digested event, a finished event, a known event; it may take flight if it so wishes or it may find a nest. It does not bother us anymore and it does not matter.

The second one, what an imprecision of love or light only half achieved? It was a guessed secret which we liked because of its sensuality and it hurt us because of the frustration of our clean hope.

The third one left us as soon as we came to know it. But we knew that perhaps it would return; that it would return as the fourth.

The fifth layer, the fifth layer! Is this the deep? It is made out of corpses of our dreams, of the dark and earthy chunks of our lives, of the flesh and soul mixed with white plaster; these are the fragments of our death poisoning us with their metamorphic, eternal mystery. We will only know each afterwards of their metamorphosis.

3.

Warrior of Light

The unmatching, blue beauty of this other midday, just like the one over there, from there and complete here, is, because of its uniqueness, also universal. This midday, like the other one, is also the whole midday, the whole day, by itself like the universe. The universe is a whole blue day.

I, electric spring of warm flesh, send rays to the infinite space; the electric space, empty of figures, sends back its rays towards my infinity.

It is a war of light, of love and beauty that lasts for a moment like a warrior of peace and tender pain, in the front or back of the center of the world: a world without names, differences or disproportions.

4.

In Vain

Within this immense sea of the earth, the cities: one, another, nearer, further. Within them, legs and arms, eyes, ears, noses, mouths that move incessantly, that flee, that come, that listen, that grab, that smell, look, eat and drink, that talk, that see, that shout, that move incessantly. From among all those there appear the ones of one particular person or thing with absolute prominence.

Those arms, etc., do not move in search of a positive dream, or to be seen by the one specially desired, etc., in a unique way; but only to be grabbed, etc., by anyone in any way.

That bravery of the arms and that resistance of the legs, this and that and that other move of the mouth, of the nose, etc., what has the most taste, what is best for the mind, all that is in vain. They are not able to lose a step and chase after the specially desired and lived in the absolute.

III

"This is what I want: not to be someone else. I want to be who I am, as I am now, a woman seventeen years old, and this wherever I might be."

"I understand, now, why in this village everyone says you have a name for being weird, some more, others less!"

"I have a clean conscience, though. I treat everyone the same and I understand of everyone what I think is their best. What I think is wrong I pay no attention to. In this way I keep from everyone what is best for me. They, on the other hand, some more, others less, as you said, seem to see in me only what they do not understand or do not like. They tell me I will forever live alone. I do not understand why. I do not feel alone. Even the weirdest people interest me. You must have heard people talk about Don Perro Pachon. This man arrived here from no one knows where, and he has no family. He lived on very little and did not steal or beg. He had a flat-nosed dog that barked at everyone. One day the dog disappeared and the poor man started to talk as if he were barking. People used to say in jest: 'He has inhabited the dog's body to save a meal.' Even before that happened he had something of a dog in his talk, his growl, his gestures. He wanted no one hear him. He withdrew more and more into a corner; now he looks like a dog. People say the dog ate him up as punishment. But he does not bark at me. He lets me get near him. He even visits me sometimes. There is something in him I do not understand but I like; something to do with his past and his memories. If I am to be honest, Don Perro Pachon entertains me more than anyone else."

"I think it's wonderful."

"I am telling you more than I should, though. I let myself go. I like to let myself go like our river. To let myself go is my way of life. But then people laugh at me, or become serious in front of me, or correct me, or leave me alone. I do not like being left alone. I like people. I told you they all have something I like!"

IV

Between an Opening and a Closing

The world split open through the round flesh of a mother, an oven, not a pit, and a new being came to life; his dark eyes opened by lightning to the flame of a round, red and black sun and embraced the immensity.

But as those eyes opened fear opened in that child too, the fear that those eyes would end up closing (like dark, one-day flowers) to life, this only life; this life: a fear born between an opening and a closing of a pair of eyes!

This being, this tiny animal from the deep, called himself many names that no one knows the meaning of. This is exactly what I call myself today, and these eyes of mine are his own!

This name is my own name; these eyes of mine are his own, frightened eyes. From this fright springs life, between an opening and a closing of those two eyes.

V

The Light of the World of Life

If a man were to pay exact attention to the light of the
world upon his land, to all that funeral absence, the speeding
distance, the eternal impossibility that the light of the world
sheds on his life (shining splendor that moves him about
bewitched in its magic), then he would be unable to live unless
he burnt each day, unless he melted himself into light. This
beautiful, deeply sad farce of the world's light upon life, is it
because the light comes from so far away? Shore, ripple wave
of light springing from a center we are unable to locate or
catch, that we will never catch or locate!

Fields, seas, villages, rivers, roads of the earth bathed in
light of the external infinite. Beauty and ugliness, mediocrity
and human heights under the complete, absent light! What a
confusion of life under the light of the world; what an
outpouring of all solid liquid, gaseous putrefactions; what lack
of balance! Every shout upon the earth turns under the light of
the world, no matter how happy its origin, into a shout of
horror, surprise, condolence, anguish, despair, hate.

And you, drunk with whatever, you who stumbling on the
tile of the sidewalk grab at the whitewash with the slippery
light of the world, why do you reach out so secure but because
of the impossible security of the light of the world reflecting on
white? And you, masks fleeing the February of life to lighted
squares on town halls, to greasy poles with the late light of the
world in the pocket at the top, why do you run, climb, descend
burning poles, but to reach the false ends of the light of the
world at the top of the pole in the square? Mad, stupid, sick

people who when the light of the world strikes you, you all stick out exaggerated faces to others; what is it that runs through your poor brains of a different gray but the light of the world on the earth, this light of the strange infinity of life, this light of the great world in a hole, the emptiness of your high, small depths? And you isolated, rinsed white, broken women dressed in black, getting hoarse shouting at a naked child who runs dirty or dressed in rags and tumbles over the setting light of the edges of the world, to whom do you shout but to the light of the forgotten of the world upon the dust?

The light of the world is life: incomprehensible fear, jest, howl, irony. Everything and all, love and death, war and peace is covered by it, looking so black, everyone so black. Why, for what reason is there such blinding clarity? Who, what focuses on us thus and looks at us, soulless, sold out, lost, in this manner?

Is this the sublime gift that everything else presents to the poet, to be able to see this sun shine, this moon light, this lake of the light of the world upon the earth? Brave, poor poet, you alone face the impossible light, you open it up with your eager fingers, you, at times, burn up in the all with no things, in the gold of black things and return, your hair gray with strange ashes!

VI

It Is Not Yet Today

I wish to do this and that and that!

All the enthusiasm and joy from within spring thus before me, as if my blood were made of light and I were a green, millenial pinetree turned once more white-gold with a spring dawn. The true day of my life opens up like a long day without night, eternal (death is nothing for the one who works, dreams and sings): the beautiful morning holds up, the midday is eternal plenitude, the immense afternoon is wide open. . . .

My everyday life! Always the same: green pine tree, its burning top filled with high birds, always more!

As in those pre-days of the day (an early morning trip, an early awakening) when the body feels strong and the soul is ready for later on and we tell ourselves excited: "Today I will do this and that and that!" And it is already today (and we are doing everything), a blue and pink today upon the western, white walls transparent with futures, and we are already enjoying it. . . .

And yet, it is not yet today.

VII

From There

    You are asking me with words from here. This, however, you should ask me with words from there.

    (From there? Where from is there? I do not know from where is there!)

    Words from there, where whoever lives there, out of a wish from his god, who is not mine, lives over a field with a different light, in a house of a different color.

VIII

Tree and Face

That solid almond tree (unknown against a unique western sky crowned with the lean sickle of the universal moon) begins to look as if it were mine due to its complete blackness.

That still profile of that face of that unknown and different woman (outlined against the tree trunk with the last green light) is beginning to look familiar, familiar. . . .

It looks familiar through a superior knowledge. It looks the same, yet different, as it came to me a thousand centuries ago.

IX

Happenings

1.

The Truth

I said I had the truth. Suddenly someone came in, talked about some other thing and the truth escaped me to its world of forgetfulness.

Now, I am unable, due to my poor memory, to remember the truth. This much is clear: I live in a lie.

2.

I Caught It

Juanito, who keeps asking questions and is only three years old, with intense brown eyes, his color faded, his face to one side, is asking his beautiful mother for the millionth time, hoping she will look at him directly: "Mama Pura, where is God?"

"My son, you are such a nuisance. I have told you many times that God is everywhere!"

"Yes, but before He was there, where was He?"

"My son, there you go again. You already know. I have told you many times, stop!"

"Then, God is here, and here and here!" He would then point to the metal bulb at the end of the banister, to the rose-plaster in the center of the empty ceiling, to the bird cage of the parrot, to the wash basin. His mother would say: "Yes son, yes son, yes son!"

"And here, inside of this water glass also?"

"Yes, son of god, inside of that glass too!"

Juanito, then, turned the glass suddenly down upon the table and shouted:

"I caught it!"

3.

"Meaning To"

Did you really "mean to" do it? Yes, I did; you always do as you are always "meaning to." You mean harm. You do not mean well.

The patio for the merienda, filled in its free hour, is beginning to look unpleasant, the opposite of what it was meant to be.

Young bodies move here and there, souls peak at each other pitifully, trying to find amusement in the flowers.

Two pairs of eyes faced each other: "Did you mean to? You'll be sorry!" Then the guilt, laughter and tears, running away, trying to appear indifferent yet loaded with that other thing, all of that other thing, the exact thing, the vulgar thing, alas, the true thing.

Yes, it was a quick journey from the impossible, dreamed paradise to the ordinary daily bread.

4.

That Little Witch

Would it be possible to place it? That gesture, the gesture of that little girl dressed in mourning, the thin, bony, cute, dusty, dirty girl . . . . That little witch, said who?

Was it in that twisted alleyway, under that dry tree, on that broken-down car that was leaving?

It was a gesture of vengeful mockery; the mouth smirked towards the left eye, the face twisted to form an 's'; it was a gesture supported by the round shoulder, running through the tiny waistline and ending in her foot. It was the gesture of an outcast, a charming little outcast. That little witch, that gesture. . .!

"Ah, yes, yes, yes! It was at the Puerto de Santa María, while studying with the Jesuits. No, it was not a girl; it was a boy . . . an 'extern' and his name was. . . ."

X

The Complete End

Smoke climbed slowly and the falling sun was coloring it through with tones which became melodiously lost. The smoke vanished with the disappearing tones.

I, surrendering to an overpowering pantheism, became the exit for the light, a metamorphosis of descending color, smoke flying away from me. Sun, smoke and I were a fatal column of silent hopelessness.

Suddenly the sun set, the smoke became clean and I disappeared. The whole world died. The complete end had arrived. The complete end had arrived with the end of just one thing, a thing that was almost nothing, an emanation, smoke only.

XI

Boni, the Stepdaughter

(Córdoba)

From the time her father remarried she became a daughter to her stepmother and her stepmother a mother to her. She was given the best room, the best furniture, the best dresses, the best seat at the table. Affectionate gestures and pampering were constant on her:

"Boy, have respect for your sister!"

"Girl, go with your sister!"

"Love your sister very much!"

The children: "Sister Boni, sister Boni!"

She was the only one going by the name of sister. Carmen was called Carmen. But she became sister Boni.

Luisito was allowed, sometimes, as an honor to the infant, to sleep in sister Boni's room. The doctor was constantly visiting her. She was given the best desserts and the best medicines. When she became engaged, the stepmother guided and advised her as if she were her own daughter. When she got married the arrangements became more elaborate than for any other occasion. Everything was brought from the city.

Once married and with children, her stepmother's house became the end of her walks. Her children were more spoiled than those of the other children.

When the mother (and stepmother) was coming to her own end, all the children gathered in the room of her agony. The dying woman had been silent and smiling to herself that whole afternoon. When Boni entered the room the stepmother

opened her eyes and turned them towards another side, as if
she suddenly were looking at someone she had never seen
before. With a deep voice she said:

"You, son of a bitch. . .!"

Then . . . She died in holiness, seriously, as she had
always lived.

XII

The Color of the World

Man is born, looks around and sees, when the light permits, the color of the world.

What is that being in relation to the color of the world?

The color of the world, is it greater than the feeling of the man who was a child?

Was I not born to see, feel, express the color of the world?

They blame me for the color of the world! Isn't the world just color (light and color, color and shadow, shape and color, color and vagueness?)

When I name color I first name spirit, then shape, and then everything else.

Let everything disappear in the face of the color of the world.

Color of the world, then silence. Then . . . then my death. The color of the world has come to an end.

(1919)

XIII

A Woman's Gesture

Where lies that unique gesture, that imponderable, isolated gesture which thus lingers in my feverish imagination as I settle within these arythmic, gray, thirsty days of my new arrival from there? The background flees and vanishes, again and again, as a scene between mountains which is almost seen as if within a dream from within a train. The gesture endures, unattainable. Sadness knows it is still fixed on that moment, where it was, with the exactness of a statute at the brink of an abyss.

(Was it on that landing of the stairs, lighted during the day, appearing amidst the shock, the torn papers, the hesitation of a possible, very distant drama? Or was it on that immense panorama, against the stony, white curtain of the evening rain falling through that huge opening in the mauve cloud, a moving continent across a yellow sky and the horizon of an earthly sea? Or was it with the arrival of the twelve o'clock sun from the docks into a hotel with no mail, noisy with light, tables and chairs, voices from the South, sounds and dissonances from the street; was it upon that transparent line of trees and smoke against the horizontal sun of autumn's five in the afternoon; or was it under the tree with enormous black bulls walking in profile against that higher sky riding joyful, pink, tiny clouds?)

That gesture endures in me like a mute pain, beautiful, alone, alive. My brain tries in vain to seize it, bring it out from the clutter that the revolution of facts pile up; but it becomes larger each instant on the other side of the factual. My hand

tries in vain to rescue it from the precipice where, white and pale, it must fall completely and forever. Its beauty, its virtue, its grace, its perfection will not save it from the noisy, automatic, black-green cover of the well of annihilation.
(1925)

XIV

Spring

We seem to reproduce briefly in spring all of our being;
the whole metamorphosis of our being, matter and spirit takes
over before it takes on a definitive human form. It is the great
joy of returning to being all we have been that lights us up from
the early morning when birds, identical to the birds we were,
speak to us in that old idiom we almost understand again, of
our dreams to become men.

We come out of the free life and we recognize everything
as ours. We love, as our own, the wet, tiny stones, the smell of
yolks, herbs, flowers; we remember them as belonging to us.
Our voice takes on unexpected accents of water, wind, forest.
Between the branches of our legs runs the water. Our glances
are as beautiful as flowers; our chest, mouth are like fruits; our
movements become easy with the undulation of the air or a
branch.

We stop, like a tree, by the shore. The water smiles back
with our own smile. Within us the birds sing as they used to
when we were trees. We, too, sing with the confidence of the
water and the birds. We are a condensed spring. Its birth
causes our rebirth. She extracts us from everything we were
before we became human flesh; she springs us in everything as
she does herself. Our clothes become excessive, so we throw
them away. We caress our bodies with the exalted, joyful
sensuality of the true life, the life of pure green, of clean blue,
and live gold.
(1933)

XV

Subject, Mummy, Object

I died. They undressed me from my clothes of being alive, they washed me, covered me with ointments, wrapped me up in sheets for the dead, painted a face over my own and left me in a tomb, my new home, as an invitation to the gods for all eternity.

Time knows how long I dwelt there in that house, getting used to it, taking possession of my new being which I considered to be the definitive one, I who had become the whole and the nothingness for eternity. I fell so much in love with my new life that for nothing, and in no way, would I have ever wished to return to the surface. What went on over me seemed to me to be a matter for the air. The sky knows it was my daily earth before. That before it was eternity. I was calm under the sky that was my earth. Now I am immortal and men are the mortal ones.

Now, suddenly, some other men from other skies different from mine have taken me out of my house which I thought would be eternal. The sun has warmed me as it always did during my life above on my painted face, and its warmth traversing through my face of cloth, rubber and paint, has reached my erased face. They took me, then, with care to some unknown place, removed my painted face, the clothes wrapped around me, washed the dry and hard ointments and left me naked again. They, then, elaborately worked on my body and put everything back on as close as possible to how it looked before and placed me in this display case, where I am now a spectacle to all in this museum of the past.

There is no doubt I have gone through a resurrection. Am I at the same time, and for how long, in the future, in the heavens, in eternity and so on? Or is this the beginning for me of my resurrected life? Where will I end? Am I safer in this museum than I was under the earth? Why did they move me from my definitive security? How long will it last? All those people living their first life, their daily life, are they able to see me and understand what, after all, eternity is for a king whom other men considered to be a god?
(1940)

XVI

Dry Blood

A beautiful lily-white woman from Maryland presented me on Christmas night, the same night as my birthday, with a magnificent, nameless, white flower. It was one of those flowers that lasts, lives only, one single night.

"A curse on you, woman," I said. "Why did you not think before you plucked it, about all the things this beautiful flower had to do on this beautiful night of her only life? And now, what am I going to do with her, not knowing herneeds or her wishes?"

I set the flower on the ground in the garden. The following morning I found only a stain of dry blood on the grass.
(1945)

XVII

The World, in Order to Be One, Eats Itself Up

The world is one because it eats itself. And on what else would it be able to live, or rather die?

That boasted unity, poets, is only death (only death). All the signs of the world are only death. Death is, therefore, poetry.

What a terrible lie, universal lie (of the universe)! What a frightening, natural crime!

How can we punish the criminals? What else do they do but follow the world's example? What are they but helpers of unity?

Criminals are the most natural beings of the natural crime of the world. They just slow down the rhythm.

The savage is the true poet and the true scientist.

Unity needs war. War is the search for unity, universal unity. That is why there is war. That is why war is natural.

Peace is putrefaction, decadence, stupor; it is dead life.

The death of war is life dead.

Life is death in the same proportion that death is life. This is the world's balance, the balance of the unity of the world.

Death is, therefore, half, one half; life, therefore, the other half.

For this reason it is impossible to avoid the death of life.

Love, death is my death, as much as life is my life!
(1946?)

XVIII

The Doctor

From the age of nineteen, the doctor became as necessary to him as eating or sleeping; even more he was not able to sleep or eat without his relative presence. What mysterious, inscrutable mystery had enveloped him from the beginning of the world (God only knows from where or when) and which upon the death of his father had decidedly overcome him like an invasion, or the breaking of a dike, or of a flower, or like a new birth?

During those days he was able to do everything, dared everything, was capable of everything as long as the doctor was within sight or sound. He could even dare those things that are most dangerous to life. It was not, therefore, a problem of death, but of death without the doctor. If the doctor were not near or about to arrive, his runaway pulse would rise into the hundreds, his heart would almost race out of his mouth, his body would be covered all over with cold sweat, he would surrender to a desperate unconscious.

I repeat, as a matter of fact, death was not the most grave thing that could happen to him; the grave thing would be to die without a doctor that would order him to die, as others have need of a confessor to save their lives. With the doctor nearby he did not mind dying in life. He, therefore, decided to be buried next to the doctor. When his doctor friend X died he bought a neighboring tomb, not necessarily the next one. It was sufficient that they be neighbors. He did not want a doctor constantly present, annoying, a witness of all of his life. He needed a doctor only in case of a natural or induced accident.

He died with a doctor and was buried next to a doctor. If he did not mind being dead while being alive with a doctor, he minded even less being dead in death with a dead doctor. Only that when dying he felt a deep anxiety. What if the neighboring doctor were transferred to the Pantheon for Illustrious Men, since he was an illustrious man?

He should have foreseen such an eventuality and made reservations for himself in the Pantheon for Illustrious Men, as it was offered to him by the Royal Spanish Academy.

He died with another unexpected anxiety, thinking: "What could happen to me if they transferred the dead doctor? Will I then resurrect without a doctor and live a miserable life, just because of this? And to think how well I was going to rest forever, at last, in an eternity of eternities! Will I resurrect?" (1947)

XIX

The Best Record

You, woman friend, asked me as a reproach: "What is left of the marvelously sang opera we went to this afternoon, or the extraordinary concert we listened to tonight?"

This is what is left: I have assimilated them through my spirit into my body; I have become filled with the whole thing even to the tiniest concave molecule of my being. This is what is left: that it is now mine and this has given me as much as hope, faith and charity are able to give. This is what is left: I am now better for it, my life has improved a hundredfold.

What is the use of thinking, of saying, my hard friend, that it is a pity that "that" of which nothing remains does take so much time of my life; that it would be better, perhaps, to devote that time to, say, humanity; that the record of my conscience where it remains printed can be heard by no one; and that for this reason they make those records everyone may buy in stores.

Is there a better record, my friend, than the one circling in my conscience, which keeps recording all the beautiful things of life so that I may tell them to you and you may hear them? (1949)

XX

Notes of Dry Leaves

(November)

1.

Like Two Birds

Two dry leaves coming down through the light, fall, chasing each other in waves of grace (love?), chirping like two birds.

2.

A Nose of Body and Soul

What a smell, doubly sharp, of dry leaf and green leaf rising simultaneously! What double pleasure to the nose of the body and the nose of the soul!

3.

I Have No Idea

The dry leaf of oak trees, the red of silky substance, varnished, rich, is it dry?

It is a warm mass made up of thousands upon thousands to become the untouched form of a leaf upon the ground!

No, it is not dry, it is not green. Was it green, will it become dry? I have no idea anymore how the dry looks or how the green.

4.

From the Wavy, Silver Sea

Upon a field made boundless by light, a fallen dry leaf takes from the sliding sun the silvery splendor of a wavy, peaceful sea.
(1949)

XXI

In My Natural Nest

In this house, my nest (now), on this field of this Riverdale in Maryland, one does not see the European parks or statues, nor the mythological fountains. Whatever is monumental and alien to man within an unnecessary mansion is not found here. One finds only life within its sufficient nest, as it is with the life of the numberless birds surrounding us on the grassy, seeded earth, among the elms, the cedars and maple trees, among the wild flowers. Everything here comes in the size of the house, the hut, so that everyone inside and out becomes the size of the natural.

This is a beneficent passage, rather than an obstacle, from the socially useless and disproportionate to the sufficient and proportionate phase. It is the passage from detachment to the largest, to detachment from the ordinary which forms our lives. It is a passage already on the move with counted steps to that other final nest which resides within death. If this were not so, this would make of death no more than an artificial illusion sustained by useless columns.

We shall descend thus, to the earth, step by step, not with the sudden shock of one attached to false disporportions, like mass humanity, like those with the hurry of external life. We shall first save the natural being of our naturalness within this natural nest; then within our succeeding stage of conscience; then within our free light and then take it away in our song, as within our true environment, to the last guarded peace.
(1949)

XXII

An Eye Not Seen by the World

The secret guarded within itself, gathered within itself completely, rested there.

I could catch it, open it, decipher it, make it my own; stop it from being a secret. I could make of it a visible diamond for all to see: an eye seen by the world.

But I did not want to. I threw it into the fireplace flame and watched it burn. The support of that secret, its body known to me, burnt into gold, red, blue, violet, black: all the colors of the spectrum of the secret and a few more. Then the secret itself, colorless, rose upwards by the pull of the air through the chimney's flue.

It left me, however, my secret! As a sign of gratitude, love, faith, perhaps hope, its breath, its essence. It was an essence only for myself alone: the unsayable aroma of what is totally secret, of what I am unable to say because words are not able to find its translation, not even within the music I sometimes invent.

Now, and because of it, I am the secret to be burnt, Inquisitors! I am the eye unseen by the world!
(1949)

To arrive? What is to arrive, and above all, where and what does one arrive to? How is one able to know "where" and "what" are points of arrival?

We climb a hill, we see a new horizon; a mountain, more horizon; a higher mountain, more horizon; the highest mountain, more horizon. Is that the end of everything? Have we exhausted all horizons? Every horizon seen appears different when we climb again and so is the gaze we see it with. The horizon we see on descending is different from the one we see ascending. Climber of the highest mountain, which is your ultimate horizon? Even if we could see all the horizons of this world, if that were possible, we would be left still with the moral horizons, where the total poet arrives; those are forever unending and this not because of a different gaze but because they form, they are, the limitless succession of an inextinguishable desire. Is there a height for moral life, as in love, for instance? What is the limit in the horizon for those eyes lit by love? Let him with the most languid eyes speak up! What is the last horizon of the eyes of love?
(1950)

I Broke an "L"

    I broke an "l" and a question mark with half a parenthesis closing it.

    What was it and to whom was the question directed and who could or was able or ought, or knew, how to receive it?

    Everything broke down consequently. From then on that "l" kept growing up, growing up into a lighthouse, and the half-question kept increasing, enlarging, twisted into a half-infinite seen in profile, making of itself as much of an infinite as the other half, never questioned.

    And what about the parenthesis, that half-parenthesis, larger than everything else created within the larger curve, in whose presence the not-yet-created patiently waits?

    Whose turn, then, is it now to answer?

(1952)

Books by Juan Ramón Jiménez

Almas de violeta, Madrid, 1900

Ninfeas, Madrid, 1900

Rimas, Madrid, 1902

Arias Tristes, Madrid, 1903

Jardines Lejanos, Madrid, 1904

Elegías Puras, Madrid, 1908

Elegías Intermedias, Madrid, 1909

Olvidanzas: Las Hojas verdes, Madrid, 1909

Elegías lamentables, Madrid, 1910

Baladas de Primavera (1907), Madrid, 1910

La soledad sonora (1908), Madrid, 1911

Pastorales (1905), Madrid, 1911

Poemas májicos y dolientes (1906), Madrid, 1911

Melancolía (1910–11), Madrid, 1912

Laberinto (1910–11), Madrid, 1913

Platero y Yo, Madrid, 1914

Estio (1915), Madrid, 1916

Platero y Yo (1907–17), Complete edition, Madrid, 1917

Poesías Escojidas (1899–1917), New York, 1917

Sonetos Espirituales (1914–15), Madrid, 1917

Eternidades (1916–17), Madrid, 1918

Piedra y Cielo (1917–18), Madrid, 1919

Segunda Antología Poética (1898–1918), Madrid, 1922

Poesía (1917–1923), Madrid, 1923

Belleza (1917–1923), Madrid, 1923

Canción, Madrid, 1936

La estación total, Buenos Aires, 1946

Romances de Coral Gables (1939–42), Mexico, 1948

Animal de Fondo, Buenos Aires, 1949

Tercera Antología Poética (1908–1953), Madrid, 1957

Libros de Poesías, Ed. Agustin Caballero, Madrid, 1957

Primeros Libros de Poesías, Ed. Francisco Garfias, Madrid, 1959

La corriente Infinita, Ed. Francisco Garfias, Madrid, 1961

El trabajo gustoso, Ed. Francisco Garfias, Mexico, 1961

La colina de los chopos (Madrid posible e imposible)

(1915–1924), Ed. Francisco Garfias, Barcelona, 1963

Libros inéditos de poesía, Ed. Francisco Garfias, Madrid, 1964

Dios deseado y deseante, Ed. Antonio Sanchez Barbudo, Madrid, 1964

Juan Ramón Jiménez: Antología General en Prosa, Madrid, 1978

Historias y Cuentos, Madrid, 1979

Cartas Literarias (1937–1954), Mexico, 1979

Diario de un poeta recién casado (1916), Madrid, 1917

Poesía en prosa y verso (1902–1932) Madrid, 1932

Españoles de tres mundos (1914–1940), Buenos Aires, 1942

Voces de mi copla, México, 1945

El zaratán, México, 1946

Moguer, Madrid, 1958

EDICIONES POSTUMAS (After his death)

Olvidos de Granada (1924–1928), Ed. R. Gullón, Puerto Rico 1960

Cuadernos de Juan Ramón Jiménez, Ed. F. Garfias, Madrid 1960

Por el cristal amarillo, Ed. F. Garfias, Madrid 1961

Primeras prosas, Ed. F. Garfias, Madrid 1962

Cartas (Primera Selección), Ed F. Garfias, Madrid 1962

El Modernismo, Ed. R. Gullón y E.F. Méndez, México 1962

Sevilla; Ed. F. Garfias, Sevilla 1963

Libros inéditos de poesía: I, Ed. F. Garfias, Madrid 1964

Estética y ética estética, Ed. F. Garfias, Madrid 1967

Libros inéditos de poesía:II, Ed. F. Garfias, Madrid 1967

Con el carbón del sol, Ed F. Garfias, Madrid 1973

El andrá in de su órbita; Madrid 1974; Ed F. Garfias.

En el otro costado, Ed. A. de Albornoz, Madrid 1974

Ríos que se van, Ed. P. Beltrán de Heredia, Santander 1974

Crítica paralela, Ed. A. del Villar, Madrid 1975

La obra desnuda, Ed A.. Del Villar, Sevilla 1976

Cartas literarias, Ed. F. Garrias, Barcelona 1977

Leyenda, Ed. Sánchez-Romeralo, Madrid 1978

Elejías andaluzas, Ed. A. Del Villar, Barcelona 1980

Autobiografía y artes poétiicas, Ed. A. del Villar, Madrid 1981

Prosas críticas, Ed. Pilar G. Bedate, Madrid 1981

Isla de la Simpatía, Ed. A. Díaz Quiñones y R. Sárraga, Río Piedras, P. R. 1981

Antolojia General en prosa,
Ed. A. Crespo y P. Gómez
Bedate, Madrid 1981

Poesías últimas escojidas, Ed.
A. Crespo y P. Gómez Bedate,
Madrid 1982

Política poética, Ed. G.
Bleiberg, Madrid 1982

Espacio; Ed. de A. Albornoz,
Madrid 1982

Alerta, Ed. F. J. Blasco
Pascual, Salamanca 1983

La realidad invisible; Ed. A. S.-
Romeralo, Madrid 1983

Mujer y hombre, Ed. A. Del
Villar, Madrid 1983

Guerra en España, Ed. Angel
Crespo, Madrid 1985